ROYAL FAMILY of BARODA

Gaekwad's

Anirudh Sethi

notionpress.com

INDIA · SINGAPORE · MALAYSIA

Notion Press

Old No. 38, New No. 6
McNichols Road, Chetpet
Chennai - 600 031

First Published by Notion Press 2018
Copyright © Anirudh Sethi 2018
All Rights Reserved.

ISBN 978-1-64587-978-7

This book has been published with all efforts taken to make the material error-free after the consent of the author. However, the author and the publisher do not assume and hereby disclaim any liability to any party for any loss, damage, or disruption caused by errors or omissions, whether such errors or omissions result from negligence, accident, or any other cause.

While every effort has been made to avoid any mistake or omission, this publication is being sold on the condition and understanding that neither the author nor the publishers or printers would be liable in any manner to any person by reason of any mistake or omission in this publication or for any action taken or omitted to be taken or advice rendered or accepted on the basis of this work. For any defect in printing or binding the publishers will be liable only to replace the defective copy by another copy of this work then available.

THIS BOOK OF VADODARA AND IT'S COINS

CONTENTS

1. Origin of Vadodara 7
2. Foundation of Baroda 9
3. Baroda State Flags 23
4. Farsan and Fashion 25
5. The Coin Galleries of Baroda 27
6. Historical Visit to Baroda 65
7. Some Unknown Facts 81

Gallery of Baroda *95*
Gallery Of Coins *137*

1 ORIGIN OF VADODARA

The name of the Vadodara city was revealed in the Charter 812 which depicts the existence of the city itself at that time. The history showcases the early traders and settlers who settled in the region in 812 A.D. Until 1297 the province was ruled mostly by the Hindu kings.

It is believed that in earlier times men lived at the bank of the Vishwamitri river. On the west of the great river Vishwamitri, a place called Ankottaka was situated which was progressing in the settlement, and its people lived in burnt bricks homes. The town had commercial links with the Roman Empire. In spite of richness, the frequency of the floods of the Vishwamitri shifted the inhabitants towards the southwards area, which is known today as Akthe Ota area.

The city was also known as Chanadanvati – named after its ruler, Rajput Raja Chandan. In the 2nd century, Raja Chandan wrested power from Jians. The other name possessed by the city was Viravati and Virakshetra – a land of warriors at a different point of time.

There was a beautiful place named Vatpadraka near the river's eastern bank. The village was populated with banyan trees, so it came to be known as Vatpadraka. The word was originated from the Sanskrit word – Vatodar. There was a valley of the Banyan trees which formed a canopy kind of layer.

The Jain kings took over the Ankottaka in 800 A.D. which was later taken over by Vatpadraka in 1000 A.D. The Ankottaka became prominent Jain settlement, and Vatpadraka prospered as a commercial centre. In 1298 A.D. after the establishment of Delhi Sultanate in Gujarat, Vatpadraka overshadowed Ankottaka and Afghans made Vatpadraka as their headquarters.

2 FOUNDATION OF BARODA

The city passed through the hands of the Gupta, Rashtrakuta, and Solanki dynasties. It was held by the Sultans of Delhi and Gujarat, and then the Mughals, before finally being claimed by the Marathas of the Gaekwad dynasty in the 1720s.

In 1705, the Marathas first attacked Gujarat. The Maratha officer, Damaji Gaekwad, died in 1721 and was succeeded by his nephew – Pilajirao. Baroda was founded in 1721 when Pilajirao conquered Songadh from Mughals. There were 2 Gujaratis who helped in foundation of Gaekwad Empire – Sureshwar Desai and Dala Patel. They were the key men involved in conquering Baroda in 1724 by Pilajorao. Sureshwar Pandya started working as a revenue collector for Baroda just like his father – Dabhai Pandya. Eventually, he got Dasaigiri and came to be known as Sureshwar Desai, where Dala Patel used to live at Dala Patel ni Pole.

Baroda was a former Indian State. At the time of independence in 1947, Baroda State was merged into Bombay State. Later, on May 1st 1960, the Bombay province was further divided into Gujarat State and Maharashtra State after which Baroda became a part of Gujarat officially. The history of Baroda can be very well acquainted from the glorious Gaekwads stories.

GAEKWAD MAHARAJAS OF VADODARA – BARODA

Name	Period in years
Pilaji Rao Gaekwad	1721–1732
Damaji Rao Gaekwad	1732–1768
Govind Rao Gaekwad	1768–1771
Sayaji Rao Gaekwad I	1771–1789
Manaji Rao Gaekwad	1789–1793
Govind Rao Gaekwad	1793–1800
Anand Rao Gaekwad	1800–1818
Sayaji Rao Gaekwad II	1818–1847
Ganpat Rao Gaekwad	1847–1856
Khande Rao Gaekwad	1856–1870
Malhār Rao Gaekwad	1870–1875
Maharaja Sayaji Rao III	1875–1939
Pratap Singh Gaekwad	1939–1951
Fatehsinghrao Gaekwad	1951–1988
Ranjitsinh Pratapsinh Gaekwad	1988–2012
Samarjitsingh Ranjitsinh Gaekwad	2012-Present

FAMILY TREE OF SAYAJIRAOGAEKWAD III (1875 ONWARDS)

- Sayajirao Gaekwad III
- Bajubai Gaekwad (1881–1883)
- Putlabai Gaekwad (1882–1885)

- Fatehsinhrao Gaekwad (1883–1908)
- Pratap Singh Gaekwar and two daughters
- Fatehsinghrao Gaekwad (1930–1988)
- Mrunalini Raje Gaekwad (1931) a daughter
- Premila Raje Gaekwad (1933) a son and a daughter
- Sarla Raje Gaekwad (1935) a son and a daughter
- Vasundharadevi Raje Gaekwad (1936) three sons and a daughter
- Ranjitsinh Pratapsinh Gaekwad (1938–2012)
- Samarjitsingh Gaekwad (1967)
- Alaukika Raje (1988)
- Anjana Raje (1999)
- Lalitadevi Raje Gaekwad (1939)
- Sangramsinhrao Gaekwad (1941)
- Pratapsinhrao Gaekwad (1970)
- Priyadarshini Raje Sahib Gaekwad (1975)
- Sayajirao Gaekwad (1945–1985)
- Jaisinghrao Gaekwad (1888–1923)
- Shivajirao Gaekwad (1890–1919) Two sons and a daughter
- Indira Devi (Indiraraje) (1892–1968)
- Gayatri Devi and two other daughters and two sons
- Later descendent Riya Sen and Raima Sen
- Dhairyashilrao Gaekwad (1893–1940) Three sons and two daughters

The Gaekwads trace their origins from Pune to a Maratha Kshatriya clan by the name of Matre, meaning minister. Legend has it that in the 17th Century, a prosperous farmer called Nandaji became a militant protector of cow, gaining the nickname 'GaeKaiwari' (one who protects the cows). This label stuck to the family but was simplified to Gaekwad.

Pilajirao

It was Pilajirao and another Maratha officer Kantaji Bande who first occupied Baroda in 1728. Abhay Singh, the king of Marwar and subedar of Gujarat, got Pilajirao murdered in 1732 at Dakor. His supporters evacuated Baroda which was then occupied by Abhay Singh's army. Pilajirao's son Damajirao Gaekwad II wrested Baroda back, in 1734 and it remained with the Gaekwads till independence. Pilaji was the eldest son of Jhingojirao Kerojirao Gaekwad. He was adopted by his uncle Damaji I Gaekwad (died 1721), who had been given the hereditary title of *Shamsher Bahadur* by Chhatrapati Shahu for bravery in a battle.

Damajirao II

Damajirao II fought along with SadashivraoBhau, SrimantVishwasrao, Malharrao Holker, Jayappa and Mahadji Shinde in the Third war of Panipat in 1765.

He then conquered other territories of Gujarat. After 1770, during the rule of Sayajirao Gaekwad I, Baroda became the seat of power and the residence of the Gaekwad rulers.

Khanderao Gaekwad

The 12th ruler of Baroda, Khanderao Gaekwad, was one of the most notable jewellery collectors of the 19th Century. The civic body's headquarters was named after Khanderao, and he succeeded his brother, Ganpatrao Gaekwad, in 1856. The representatives of the British Government, Colonel Barr, describes Khenderao's rule as being marked by reforms and real progress. The old portion of the Makarpura Palace was built just for the sake of Khanderao's love of the game, and he also maintained deer reserve in its neighbourhood. His passion for the jewellery cost the treasury badly. To provide clean water to Baroda, Khanderao conceived a waterway to be constructed from Narmada river to Baroda at the expense of 36 lacs INR but later the scheme was found unviable, and the money was diverted to jewellery passion. His reign was cut short by sudden illness after 14 years of his rule.

Malharrao Gaekwad

The successor of Khanderao Gaekwad was his younger brother, Malharrao Gaekwad (1870–1875). He was the youngest son of Maharaja Sayajirao Gaekwad II. The representative of British Government, Colonel Barr did not want Malharrao to succeed Khanderao because Khanderao's wife was expecting, but Maharani Jamnabai gave birth to a girl child, and Malharrao took over the reins of the Baroda. Malharrao's five-year reign was very hectic for the British as he levied irregular taxes and victimised those people who were faithful to Khanderao. Malharrao was infamously known for the 'Baroda Poisoning case'. He attempted to give poison to British resident Colonel Phayre by mixing diamond dust in the food which was consumed by Phayre. He also made it into the headlines for making the most expensive Christmas card in the world to gift a European lady of high rank. Though it never reached its destination as the Gaekwad was arrested later on.

Sayajirao Gaekwad III

The widow of Kanderao II, Maharani Jamnabai Sahib Gaekwad, later adopted a boy from the related family, who became the next ruler of Baroda State – Sayajirao Gaekwad III. Gopalrao was born in Kavlane village of Maharashtra in March 1863 and adopted and rechristened Sayajirao Gaekwad III. There were major reforms during his ruling period. His contribution towards abolishing untouchability and child marriage is still cited by historians as turning points in Indian History. His ruling period was from 1875 to 1939. He was also a key player in freedom struggle as he joined Lokmanya Tilak to destabilise the British Empire. He also allowed using Baroda as laboratory where social reforms were implemented as an experiment to determine their success in the society. As a part of the protest against child marriage, he passed a stringent law punishing the parents or guardians who married off their children before the stipulated ages. He laid seeds for co-operatives and was first to introduce 2104-Gram Panchayat bodies and 41 Nagarpalika bodies.

During his ruling, a large narrow-gauge railway network which was started in 1862 was expanded further to Dabhoi at its focal point. This railway is still the largest narrow-gauge railway network in the world. He envisioned a water supply scheme for Baroda in 1892 at Ajwa. The biggest public park of Baroda called Kamatibag, now called Sayaji Bag was the gift to Baroda by Sayajirao III.

Maharaja Sayajirao Gaekwad III was not only reformist but also the wealthiest person globally. In spite of enormous wealth, he passed through a string of personal tragedies. His wife gave him 2 daughters Bajubhai and Putlabai and a son Fatehsinhrao, and within 5 years of marriage, she died due to pregnancy-related complications. In 1885, he married Princess Gajrabai (Chimnabai II) who gave birth to 3 sons – Jaysinhrao, Shivajirao and Dhairyashilrao and a daughter Indira Raje.

Fatehsinhrao – The eldest son – died suddenly of reasons still unexplained.

Indira Raje – Daughter of Sayajirao – refused to marry Maharaja of Gwalior.

Jaysinhrao – The second son of Sayajirao – who returned from America, was injured while riding a horse and died on August 27th, 1923.

Shivajirao – Third son of Sayajirao – died on November 24, 1919, due to complications relating to influenza and pneumonia.

Dhairyashilrao – Youngest son – could not take over the reins due to protocol relating to lineage.

Pratapsinhrao, Son of Fatehsinhrao, succeeded Sayajirao III.

Pratapsinhrao Gaekwad

Maharaja Sayajirao Gaekwad III dreamt of establishing a world-class university in Baroda. His grandson - Pratapsinhrao Gaekwad, the last ruling Maharaja of Baroda, fulfilled the dream by establishing Maharaja Sayajirao University (MSU) and the Baroda Cricket Association (BCA) within his short reign. He was the president of BCA. He also set up sprawling golf course – Gujarat's first – in the Laxmi Vilas palace compound in 1941. He also settled the "Sir Sayajirao Diamond Jubilee and Memorial Trust" which still exists and caters to the educational and other needs of the people of the former Baroda State.

Pratap Singh first married the daughter of a Sardar of Kolhapur, Shanta Devi. He had eight children with her. He ignored the anti-bigamy laws that his grandfather had imposed and in 1943 took a second wife, a glamorous divorcée considered ill-suited for the exalted role of his consort, Sita Devi of Baroda. A report revealed that Pratapsinhrao had spent millions of dollars during his visit to the USA in 1928 with his wife, Sita Devi. It is believed that Pratapsinhrao had rubbed the Indian Government the wrong way when he hesitated to merge Baroda State into Indian union after independence.

Maharaja Pratapsinhrao was "deposed" by the Government of India in 1951 for his irresponsible behaviour. He then retired to Europe with his second wife, a woman of notorious reputation, and settled in Monaco. He spent his last years in London. He died in 1968 and was succeeded by his eldest son, Fateh Singh Rao Gaekwad, who had been officiated as Maharaja since 1951.

Fatehsinghrao Gaekwad

Fateh Singh Rao Gaekwad was born to Pratap Singh Gaekwad, the last ruling Maharaja of Baroda and his first wife, Maharani Shanta Devi Sahib Gaekwad. He served in public office as a Member of Parliament, Parliamentary Secretary of the Defence Ministry, MLA in Gujarat, Minister of Health, Fisheries and Jails, Chancellor of the Maharaja Sayajirao University in Baroda, and Chairman of the Board of Governors, National Institute of Sports in 1962–63. He was also the author of the book, *The Palaces of India* (1980).

As a cricketer, Gaekwad represented Baroda in the Ranji Trophy between 1946 and 1958 and had the highest score of 99 in his first season. He was an attacking right-handed batsman. He played against the touring teams on various occasions between 1948 and 1954. He was an expert cricket commentator on radio and was made an honorary life member by the MCC. Gaekwad was the President of the Board of Control for Cricket in India from 1963 to 1966, after serving as Vice-President from 1959 to 1960 and again in 1962–63. He was the manager of the Baroda Cricket Association from 1960. Known in England as "Jackie Baroda", he managed the Indian tour of England in 1959 and of Pakistan in 1978–79 and 1982–83. He still holds the record of being the youngest president of BCCI.

In the 26th amendment of the Constitution of India promulgated in 1971, the Government of India abolished all official symbols of princely India, including titles, privileges, and remuneration (privy purses).

He died in the Breach Candy Hospital in Bombay on September 1st 1988 at the age of fifty-eight, to be succeeded, as titular Maharaja of Baroda, by his younger brother, Ranjitsinhrao Gaekwad.

Ranjitsinhrao Gaekwad

Ranjitsinhrao Gaekwad was the second son of Maharaja Pratapsinhrao Gaekwad and Maharani Shantadevi. He was a member of the Lok Sabha (lower house of parliament in India) and served two terms as an MP (Member of Parliament), from 1980–89. He became the Maharaja of Baroda after the death of his elder brother on in September 1988.

Ranjitsinhrao Gaekwad was also a well-known painter. He married on December 15th 1964 to Maharani Subhangini Devi (Arunadevi Jadhav). They had 3 children – 2 daughters and 1 son, Yuvraj Samarjit Singh Gaekwad.

Samarjitsinh Gaekwad

Yuvraj Samarjitsinh Gaekwad was the 16th Maharaja of Baroda since 2012 (Laxmi Vilas Palace, Baroda - 390001, Gujarat, India). Born on 25th April 1967, married on 27th February 2002 in New Delhi, to Rajkumari Radhika Kumari [HH Maharani Radhikaraje Gaekwad].

3 BARODA STATE FLAGS

DURING 1874–1936

Queen Victoria granted permission to use the flag of Princely Standard from 1875 till 1936.

This flag represented a sword held with four-fingered hand, risen from the crown-like shape.

DURING 1936–1949

In 1936, the Princely Standard was changed to Tudor inspired Crown at top and Scimitar or Sword (Tulwar) below, which was used till 1949.

NATIVE STATE RED ENSIGN OR MERCHANT FLAG

There was also a Native State Red Ensign used during the British Raj for the States that were not directly governed by the British, but by a local ruler through a form of indirect rule, subject to a subsidiary alliance under the paramountcy of the British Crown. Baroda State had a coastline and so, used versions of the red ensign on their merchant vessels.

The flag consists of a mounted trooper and a scimitar and the word BARODA in white on a rectangular field of red ochre with a white margin.

4 FARSAN AND FASHION

Good upmarket restaurants and street food are plentiful in Vadodara. The old city, Fatehgunj area, and Vadodara's other bazaars offer a huge variety of *farsan* or snacks. *Sevusal* is the most popular of these staple street foods, which also include *kachori, chevdo, bhakarwadi, jalebi, papdi, fafda, khaman,* and *idada*. Most of these snacks are easy on the pocket.

During a shopping spree for a *chaniya–choli* outfit and Navratri jewellery at Nava Bazaar, locals directed me to the famous Pyarelal Ki Kachori in Mangal Bazaar, a small shop doing brisk business in newsprint-wrapped kachoris stuffed with puffed rice, onion, sev, peanuts, dal, tomato, potato, chilli paste, and oozing with a sweet-and-spicy chutney.

Another local favourite is Manmohan Farsan, a hole-in-the-wall near the Kothi building. I was drawn by the whiff of frying samosas and bhajias which floats above the din of the crowd.

Snacks like chevdo and bhakarwadi are hot sellers at Shree Jagdish Farsan Mart.

Barodians snack from morning to evening. Near the railway station, Jagdish Farsan Mart starts selling its famous bhakarwadi at 6 a.m. At Duliram Peda in Raopura, a fresh batch of sweet peda is made every hour.

They complete the culinary experience with the city's sugar-tinged Gujarati thalis and the more savoury and spicier Kathiawadi thalis. The decor and Gujarati thali at the Mandap in Hotel Express Tower at Alkapuri is very attractive. A cloth mandap hangs over each table, and the food is served in copper-plated utensils. Also, in Alkapuri, Sasumaa Gujarati Thali has basic but clean interiors, and meals are served in delightful extra-large steel thalis and an array of small bowls.

Both restaurants serve delicious seasonal Gujarati vegetables, served with *bajra, narotla,* or millet rotis smeared with pure ghee. Only dal and *kadhi* are sweetened, and for fussy eaters, there are Punjabi versions of each dish.

Search for an authentic Kathiawadi thali leads to Kismat Kathiawadi Dhaba on NH8, replete with charpais but for a more comfortable dining experience visit Shree Kathiyawadi Khadki's new, air-conditioned restaurant in Sharnam Fortune Mall on Racecourse Road. It serves Gujarati thalis and Kathiawadi à la carte in the evening.

Shiv Shakti Kathiawadi Hotel near the Vishwamitri Bridge opposite a Mahindra tractor shop is equally popular for churma ka laddoo. The laddoo is made on alternate days and is in high demand. Both restaurants serve the Kathiawadi specialities of sev-tametanu shaak, ringannu bhartu, masala khichdi kadhi, dhokla, bajra and makaina rotla, and of course, chaas and papad.

5 THE COIN GALLERIES OF BARODA

HISTORY

History of coins struck by Gaekwad rulers divides itself into two periods. The 1st period roughly begins somewhere after 1763, and it ends in the year 1802. This period roughly corresponds with the reign of Emperor Shaha Alum of Delhi (1759–1806), and it covers the reigns of Sayajirao I (1773–93) and his two regents Fatehsinhrao and Baba Sahib (1778–89) and Manajirao (1789–93). Govindrao's claims (1793–1800) were recognised prior to 1771. But soon they were set at nought, and they were recognised again in 1793. He died in 1800. Coins that can be unmistakably attributed to Sayajirao I, his two regents or to Govindrao are not known. Nevertheless there is ample evidence in the State records which establishes beyond doubt, that coins were struck by these Gaekwad rulers except Manajirao during these periods. Three copper coins struck at Baroda in the year 1802 and 1804, are in the Lahore Museum. They are Shaha Alum-type with a dagger and mint name of Baroda inscribed on it. Regnal years of Shah Alum are mentioned on them. The type of coin struck by the earlier Gaekwad rulers probably resembled the type issued by other Maratha rulers of this period.

INCEPTION:

In India British issued coins between 1835 and 1947. The coins issued between 1835 and 1858 was struck under the authority of East India Company. Coins issued between 1862 and 1947 was struck under the Authority of Crown, also known as Regal issue.

Coins issued between 1835 and 1947 carried a portrait of the crowned emperor/empress of England. Coinage during this period was termed as Imperial Coinage or Uniform coinage. During this period the coins were issued uniformly to all of India including Pakistan, Bangladesh and Burma.

Coins during British rule was minted from the following mints across India:

1. Madras Mint: It was set up in 1640 and was closed by 14th Aug 1869
2. Bombay Mint: It was set up in 1671
3. Calcutta Mint: It was set up in 1759

After achieving independence on 15th August 1947, the monetary system remained unchanged during the transition. The first post-independence coin was issued on 15th August 1950.

THE ANNA SERIES:

Monetary System Anna Series

	1 Pice
4 Pice	1 Anna
16 Annas	1 Rupee

The Anna system was followed during the transition period up to 1957. The Anna was introduced on 15th August 1950. In this coinage, the bust of the King was replaced with the figure of Sarnath Capital of Ashoka also known as the Ashoka Lion Capital, as insignia of Republic India.

THE DECIMAL SERIES:

Monetary System Anna Series	
100 Paisa	1 Rupee

The move towards decimalisation was afoot for over a century. However, it was in September 1955 that the Indian Coinage Act was amended for the country to adopt a metric system for coinage. The Act was enforced on April 1st, 1957. The rupee remained unchanged in value and nomenclature.

During 60s small denomination coins, which were made of bronze, nickel-brass, cupro-Nickel and Aluminium Bronze, were gradually minted in Aluminium. This change commenced with the introduction of the new hexagonal 3 paise coin.

1, 2, and 3 paisa coins were discontinued in the 70s. Stainless steel coinage of 10, 25 and 50 paise were introduced in 1988 and of one rupee in 1992. The Government of India issues 3 basic coins:

1. Circulating Coins: These coins are the most commonly seen among the public. This is for public circulation. Not much care is taken while minting these coins.
2. Uncirculated Coins: Also, generally known as UNC (uncirculated). These coins are minted for collection purpose and not for general circulation. These coins are minted with special care and come with special packing.
3. Proof Coins: Like UNC coins, these are also issued for collection and not for general circulation. As compared to UNC, these coins are much sharper and highest care is given at every stage of minting.

Although the Gaekwads trace their origins to this time, it was not until considerably later, that Baroda can be truly thought of as an independent State. The first coins issued by the Gaekwads were issued by Manaji Rao (ruled 1789–93), and they followed the Maratha pattern of naming the Mughal emperor Shah Alam II, distinguishing themselves only by the placement of an extra mark or letter to indicate the issuer. Manaji, for example, placed a Nagari letter *ma* on his coins.

After 1857, since the Mughal emperor had been deposed even formally, it no longer made any sense to issue coins under his name, so the designs were changed, and coins were issued in the name of "the Commander of the Sovereign Band," a title of the Gaekwad. The legends on these coins were still in Persian, and the coins themselves were still hand-struck. Finally, in stages during the 1870s, Nagari legends and different designs were introduced and also milled coins began to be issued, eventually featuring the portrait of the Gaekwad on them.

Anand Rao (1800–1819)

Anand Rao: Silver 1/2 rupee in the name of Shah Alam II, Ahmedabad
Weight: 5.78 gm.
Diameter: 17–18 mm
Die axis: 11 o'clock
Legend, naming Shah Alam/Legend, including Ahmedabad mintmark of *ankus* (elephant goad) in the *julus* and Nagari *ga*
Reference: KM C18

Anand Rao: Silver 1/2 rupee in the name of Shah Alam II, Ahmedabad
Weight: 5.78 gm.
Diameter: 17–18 mm
Die axis: 11 o'clock
Legend, naming Shah Alam/Legend, including Ahmedabad mintmark of *ankus* (elephant goad) in the *julus* and Nagari *ga*
Reference: KM C18
The Nagari *ga* on this coin may have stood for "Gaekwad," but it was used in this form only on Anand Rao's Ahmedabad coinage.

Anand Rao (1800–1819)

Anand Rao: Silver 1/2 rupee in the name of Muhammad Akbar II, Baroda
Weight: 5.67 gm.
Diameter: 17–18 mm
Die axis: 3 o'clock
Legend, including Baroda mintmark of a curved sword (or scimitar) in the *julus* and Nagari *aa*
Reference: KM C26

Although Muhammad Akbar's name is off the flan, we can identify this coin by a particular form of Nagari *aa* (we see just the tip of the letter on the right edge of the flan on the reverse). This form was used only on Anand Rao's Baroda coins in the name of Muhammad Akbar II. On this coin, we also see the curved sword or scimitar, the dynastic symbol of the Gaekwads.

Sayaji Rao II (1819–1847)

Sayaji Rao II: Silver rupee in the name of Muhammad Akbar II, Baroda, AH 1238, RY 18
Weight: 11.46 gm.
Diameter: 22 mm
Die axis: 12 o'clock
Legend naming Muhammad Akbar II, AH date 1238 (= 1822–23 CE)/
Legend, with scimitar *left* of the *julus*, RY date 18, Nagari *sa* (for Sayaji)
Reference: KM C38.1

The coinage of Sayaji Rao II had three phases, most easily distinguished by the position of the scimitar on the reverse side. This coin belongs to the first phase, where the scimitar is represented vertically to the left of the *julus*, in continuation of the position in which it was represented on the coinage of Anand Rao (see the previous coin).

Sayaji Rao II (1819–1847)

Sayaji Rao II: Silver 1/2 rupee in the name of Muhammad Akbar II, Baroda,
AH 1244, RY 24
Weight: 5.72 gm.
Diameter: 16 mm
Die axis: 8 o'clock
Legend naming Muhammad Akbar II,
AH date 1244 (= 1828–29 CE)/
Legend, with scimitar above the julus, RY date 24,
Nagari sa off flan
Reference: KM C37.2

This coin belongs to the second phase of Sayaji Rao's coinage, where the scimitar is represented horizontally above the julus. KM lists the RY 24 half rupees with AH date 124x, indicating the lack of a specimen that showed the AH date clearly. This coin clearly shows the AH date of 1244, yielding the combination 1244/24, which is known in the rupee denomination of this type.

Sayaji Rao II: Silver 1/2 rupee in the name of Muhammad Akbar II, Baroda, RY 27
Weight: 5.67 gm.
Diameter: 16 mm
Die axis: 6 o'clock
Legend naming Muhammad Akbar II,
AH date off flan/
Legend, with scimitar above the julus, RY date 27,
Nagari sa (for Sayaji)
Reference: KM C37.2

This coin shows the Nagari sa, which was off the flan on the previous specimen.

Sayaji Rao II (1819–1847)

Sayaji Rao II: Silver rupee in the name of Muhammad Akbar II, Baroda, RY 36
Weight: 11.51 gm.
Diameter: 21 mm
Die axis: 8 o'clock
Legend naming Muhammad Akbar II, AH date off flan/Legend, with scimitar to right of the julus, RY date 36 (= 1840–41 CE), Nagari sa (for Sayaji)
Reference: KM C38.3

This coin belongs to the third phase of Sayaji's coinage, where the scimitar is represented vertically to the right of the julus.

Sayaji Rao II: Copper paisa in the name of Muhammad Akbar II, Baroda, sword type,
AH 1236/RY 16
Weight: 11.16 gm.
Diameter: 20 mm
Die axis: 9 o'clock
Legend naming Muhammad Akbar II,
AH date 1236 (= 1820–21 CE)/
Legend, with scimitar to the left of the julus, RY date 16, Nagari sa (for Sayaji)
Reference: KM C33.1

Sayaji Rao's Baroda paisas form the most interesting series. There is a whole series of different symbols featured on the reverse. This coin features a scimitar.

Sayaji Rao II: Copper 1/2 paisa in the name of Muhammad Akbar II, Baroda, sword type,
AH 1236/RY 16
Weight: 5.87 gm.
Diameter: 16 mm
Die axis: 9 o'clock
Legend naming Muhammad Akbar II,
AH date 1236 (= 1820–21 CE)/
Legend, with scimitar to the left of the julus, RY date 16, Nagari sa (for Sayaji)
Reference: KM C31.1

Sayaji Rao II (1819–1847)

The half paisa version of the previous coin. The half paisas also carried different symbols.

Sayaji Rao II: Copper paisa, Amreli, AH 1257
Weight: 6.88 gm.
Diameter: 22–23 mm
Die axis: 11 o'clock
Devanagari letters sa, ga with scimitar below, all within dotted border/
Legend, including AH date 1257 (= 1841–42 CE)
Reference: KM C29.6

The Amreli paisas had a very different fabric. The reverse of this coin is clearly overstruck.

Ganpat Rao (1847–1856)

Ganpat Rao: Copper paisa, Amreli, AH 1257
Weight: 6.40 gm.
Diameter: 21–23 mm
Die axis: 4 o'clock
Devanagari letters 'Sri' above and gaga below, with a flower in the centre, leaf at left and scimitar at right, all within ruled and inward-rayed border/Legend
Reference: KM C39

Khande Rao (1856–1870)

Khande Rao: Copper paisa, Amreli, AH 1277
Weight: 5.76 gm.
Diameter: 20 mm
Die axis: 3 o'clock
Devanagari letters Sri above and kha ga below, with leaf sprig in the centre, flower at left and scimitar at right, all within ruled and inward-rayed border/
Legend, including AH date 1277 (= 1860–61 CE)
Reference: KM Y1

Khande Rao (1856–1870)

Khande Rao: Copper paisa, Amreli, AH 1277
Weight: 6.27 gm.
Diameter: 18 mm
Die axis: 2 o'clock
Devanagari letters Sri above and kha ga below, with leaf sprig in the centre, flower at left and scimitar at right, all within ruled and inward-rayed border/Legend, including AH date 1277 (= 1860–61 CE)
Reference: KM Y1

Malhār Rao (1870–1875)

Malhār Rao Silver rupee, Baroda Mint, AH 1288
Weight: 11.47 gm.
Diameter: 20 mm
Die axis: 6 o'clock
Legend/Remnants of Persian legend, scimitar at left, Nagari maagaa (for Malhār Rao), AH date 1288 (= 1871–72 CE) below.
Reference: KM Y21

It is interesting to see how the Persian legend on the reverse of Malhār Rao's coinage has been shunted aside; pride of place is given to the Nagari letters identifying the king, the scimitar, and the AH date, which has migrated to the reverse.

Malhār Rao Silver 1/2 rupee, Baroda Mint, AH 1288
Weight: 5.68 gm.
Diameter: 15 mm
Die axis: 1 o'clock
Legend/Remnants of Persian legend, scimitar at left, Nagari maagaa (for Malhār Rao), AH date 1288 (= 1871–72 CE) below.
Reference: KM Y20

The half rupees are scarcer than the full rupees.

Malhār Rao (1870–1875)

Malhār Rao Copper double paisa, Baroda Mint, AH 1289 Weight: 15.45 gm.
Diameter: 20–21 mm
Die axis: 1 o'clock
Legend/Nagari maagaa (for Malhār Rao), sphere or circle below, flanked by AH date 1289 (= 1872–73 CE), scimitar below.
Reference: KM Y17

Malhār Rao's copper coinage continued featuring the shaded ball or circle seen on the late coins of Sayaji Rao II.

Malhār Rao Copper paisa, Baroda Mint, AH 1288
Weight: 7.73 gm.
Diameter: 19–21 mm
Die axis: 9 o'clock
Legend/Nagari maagaa (for Malhār Rao), sphere or circle below, flanked by AH date 1288 (= 1871–72 CE), scimitar below.
Reference: KM Y16

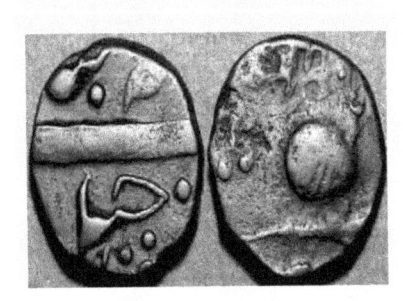

Malhār Rao Copper paisa, Baroda Mint, AH 1288
Weight: 3.85 gm.
Diameter: 15 mm
Die axis: 12 o'clock
Legend/Nagari maagaa (for Malhār Rao), sphere or circle below, flanked by AH date (not visible), scimitar below.
Reference: KM Y15

Sayaji Rao III (1875–1938)

Sayaji Rao III: Silver rupee, Baroda Mint, error date?
Weight: 10.79 gm.
Diameter: 20 mm
Die axis: 9 o'clock
Legend/Remnants of Persian legend, scimitar at left, Nagari saagaa (for Sayaji Rao III), date 87 (!!) below.
Reference: KM Y29

The most unusual coin, awaiting an explanation! The position of the scimitar and the letters saagaa on the reverse identify the coin as coin of Sayaji Rao III. However, his hammered coinage carries a full AH date on the reverse and includes only the dates 1292–1302. This coin carries only the date 87. If it were shorthand for AH 1287, the date is 5 years too early for the reign of Sayaji Rao III! Another possibility is that the coin was issued by Malhār Rao in the first year of his reign (AH 1287), but his coins also normally carry a full AH date and, in any case, it seems almost certain that the Nagari letter identifying the king is saa, not maa. So perhaps this is an error date, or some other explanation is required.

Sayaji Rao III: Silver rupee, Baroda Mint, VS 1955
Weight: 11.37 gm.
Diameter: 28 mm
Die axis: 12 o'clock
Bust of the King right, wearing a jewelled turban, Nagari legend around:
srisayajirao/ma. Gaekwad/
Nagari denomination in two lines: ek/rupaya, sword, and VS date 1955 (= 1897 CE) below, wreath around Reference: KM Y36a

Portrait coins were introduced for the first time in the gold series in VS 1942 and in the silver series in VS 1948. Note the discarding of AH dates, replaced by dating in the Vikram era of 57 BCE.

Sayaji Rao III (1875–1938)

Sayaji Rao III: Copper double paisa, heavy type, Baroda, VS 1944
Weight: 16.33 gm.
Diameter: 30 mm
Die axis: 2 o'clock horses hoof, scimitar below, Nagari legend sarkar above, a circular legend in Nagari around within two dotted borders: srisayajirao.ma.gayakwad//senakhaskhelshamsher bahadur/Nagari legend naming the denomination: don paise, Nagari samvat (year) above, date 1944 (= c. 1887 CE) below, circular leaf wreath within two dotted borders around Reference: KM Y32.2

The first milled coins were produced in limited numbers towards the end of Malhār Rao's reign, but the switch took place over several years, during the 1880s. At this time, the use of Persian letters was eliminated, to be replaced by Devanagari, and entirely new designs were initiated. Also, the use of the AH date was dropped, replaced by dates in the Vikram era of 57 BCE.

The early milled coins of Sayaji Rao were heavier than the later ones; this coin is the heavy type, over 16 gm, on a large 30 mm flan, which is 3 mm thick. The letter main the obverse legend presumably stood for "Maharaj." We see the old title Shamsher Bahadur originally given to Damajirao Gaekwad in 1720, and also the title senakhaskhel, or "Commander of the Sovereign Band."

Sayaji Rao III: Copper double paisa, light type, Baroda, VS 1948
Weight: 13.05 gm.
Diameter: 30 mm
Die axis: 12 o'clock
Horse hoof, scimitar below, Nagari legend sarkar above, a circular legend in Nagari around within two dotted borders: srisayajirao.ma.gayakwad// senakhaskhelshamsher bahadur/Nagari legend naming the denomination: don paise, Nagari samvat (year) above, date 1948 (= c. 1891 CE) below, circular leaf wreath within two dotted borders around Reference: KM Y32.2a

Sayaji Rao III (1875–1938)

The weight of the copper coinage was reduced in VS 1948 (= 1891 CE), with the double paisa being cut from above 16 gm. to around 13 gm., as on this coin. The diameter of the coin was kept the same at 30 mm, but the thickness was reduced from around 3 mm. to around 2.5 mm.

Sayaji Rao III: Copper paisa, Baroda Mint, VS 1940
Weight: 7.50 gm.
Diameter: 24 mm
Die axis: 1 o'clock
Horse hoof, scimitar below, Nagari legend sarkar above, a circular legend in Nagari around within two dotted borders: srisayajirao.ma.gayakwad// senakhaskhelshamsher bahadur/Nagari legend naming the denomination: ek paisa, Nagari samvat (year) above, date 1940 (= c. 1883 CE) below, circular leaf wreath within two dotted borders around Reference: KM Y31.1

The first milled paisas of Sayaji Rao were issued in VS 1940 and had the word sarkar on the obverse in a curved configuration; this coin has that word off-centre to the left. Presumably, this coin represents one of the firsts, if not the first, dye for the new milled coinage. The die cutter had not mastered the art of centring the legend, as was achieved in all subsequent dies.

Sayaji Rao III: Copper paisa, Baroda Mint, VS 1940
Weight: 7.81 gm.
Diameter: 24 mm
Die axis: 12 o'clock
Horse hoof, scimitar below, Nagari legend sarkar above, a circular legend in Nagari around within two dotted borders: srisayajirao.ma.gayakwad// senakhaskhelshamsher bahadur/Nagari legend naming the denomination: ek paisa, Nagari samvat (year) above, date 1940 (= c. 1883 CE) below, circular leaf wreath within two dotted borders around Reference: KM Y31.1

Sayaji Rao III (1875–1938)

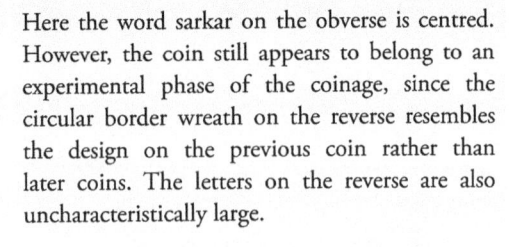

Here the word sarkar on the obverse is centred. However, the coin still appears to belong to an experimental phase of the coinage, since the circular border wreath on the reverse resembles the design on the previous coin rather than later coins. The letters on the reverse are also uncharacteristically large.

Sayaji Rao III: Copper paisa, Baroda Mint, VS 1941
Weight: 8.91 gm.
Diameter: 25 mm
Die axis: 10 o'clock
Horse hoof, scimitar below, Nagari legend sarkar above, a circular legend in Nagari around within two dotted borders: srisayajirao.ma.gayakwad// senakhaskhelshamsher bahadur/Nagari legend naming the denomination: ek paisa, Nagari samvat (year) above, date 1941 (= c. 1884 CE) below, circular leaf wreath within two dotted borders around Reference: KM Y31.1

This coin is distinguished by the obverse legend which is written in very square "boxy" letters. Also, notice how the circular wreath on the reverse border has evolved further. The scrollwork near the bottom is very different, and the flowers are now composed of four compound petals rather than the daisy-like 9–10 petalled flowers on the issues of 1940.

Sayaji Rao III: Copper paisa, Baroda Mint, VS 1947
Weight: 8.15 gm.
Diameter: 25 mm
Die axis: 2 o'clock
Horse hoof, scimitar below, Nagari legend sarkar above, a circular legend in Nagari around within two dotted borders: srisayajirao.ma.gayakwad// senakhaskhelshamsher bahadur/Nagari legend naming the denomination: ek paisa, Nagari samvat (year) above, date 1947 (= c. 1890 CE) below, circular leaf wreath within two dotted borders around Reference: KM Y31.2

Sayaji Rao III (1875–1938)

This coin represents an evolution of the Sayaji Rao paisas as to where the word sarkar on the obverse is now in a horizontal (rather than the previous curved) configuration; also, the flower and leaf wreath border on the reverse has now devolved to a simple leaf border.

The straight legend coins are divided into two broad classes: a heavyweight series of about 8.2 gm. and a lightweight series of about 6.2 gm., issued after the reform of VS 1948. This coin belongs to the heavyweight series. Further, this coin is distinguished from previous issues by the two parts of the obverse circular legend that are separated by single dots within circles. Also, the letter e in the denomination ek is "closed" rather than "open"... the second vertical line bends back towards the first, as opposed to the feature of previous issues in which the second vertical simply dangled downward without bending back.

Sayaji Rao III: Copper paisa, Baroda Mint, VS 1948
Weight: 6.18 gm.
Diameter: 25 mm
Die axis: 9 o'clock
Horse hoof, scimitar below, Nagari legend sarkar above, a circular legend in Nagari around within two dotted borders: srisayajirao.ma.gayakwad// senakhaskhelshamsher bahadur/Nagari legend naming the denomination: ek paisa, Nagari samvat (year) above, date 1948 (= c. 1891 CE) below, circular leaf wreath within two dotted borders around Reference: KM Y31.2a

This coin belongs to the later, low weight series and has a thinner planchet than the previous coin. In all other respects, it resembles the immediately preceding issues.

Curiously, the latest edition of Krause does not distinguish between the low weight series and the heavier weight coins of the earlier years (previous editions did). However, it is clear that there was a reduction of weight starting in VS 1948; this can be seen in the 2-paisa coins as well.

Sayaji Rao III (1875–1938)

Sayaji Rao III: Copper pai, Baroda Mint, VS 1944
Weight: 2.51 gm.
Diameter: 19 mm
Die axis: 1 o'clock
Horse hoof, scimitar below, Nagari legend sarkar above, a circular legend in Nagari around within two dotted borders: srigayakwad//barode/Nagari legend naming the denomination: ekpai, Nagari samvat (year) above, date 1944 (= c. 1887 CE) below, circular leaf wreath within two dotted borders around
Reference: KM Y30.2

This coin belongs to the heavyweight series. Note the shortened obverse legend because of the reduced space and the "open" e in the denomination ek.

Sayaji Rao III: Copper pai, Baroda Mint, VS 1950
Weight: 2.17 gm.
Diameter: 19 mm
Die axis: 12 o'clock
Horse hoof, scimitar below, Nagari legend sarkar above, a circular legend in Nagari around within two dotted borders: srigayakwad//baroda/Nagari legend naming the denomination: ekpai, Nagari samvat (year) above, date 1950 (= c. 1893 CE) below, circular leaf wreath within two dotted borders around Reference: KM Y30.3

This coin belongs to the low weight series. Note the "closed" e in the denomination ek and the smaller circle within which the reverse legend is crammed. Also, the rosettes separating the two parts of the obverse circular legend are bigger here, while the word sarkar is written in much smaller letters.

OTHER COINS

Princely State of Baroda – Rupee
3 Pies = 1 Pice, 4 Pices= 1 Anna, 16 Annas = 1 Rupee

½ Paisa
Copper
4.93 g
16 mm

1 Paisa - Anand Rao
(AH1215–1235/
1800–1819AD)
1225–1235 (1810–1820)
Copper, 9.76 g, 18.5 mm

1 Paisa - Anand Rao
(1810–1820)
Copper, 10.65 g, 19.3 mm

1 Paisa - Anand Rao
(1820–1848)
Copper, 10.29 g, 18.4 mm

Princely State of Baroda – Rupee
3 Pies = 1 Pice, 4 Pices = 1 Anna, 16 Annas = 1 Rupee

1 Paisa - Sayaji Rao II
(AH1235–1264/
1819–1847AD)
1240–1243 (1825–1828)
Copper, 9.80 g, 20.41 mm

1 Paisa - Ganpat Rao
(AH1264–1273/
1847–1856AD)
(1847–1856)
Copper, 9.99 g, 19.28 mm

½ Paisa - Malhar Rao
(AH1287–1292/
1870–1875AD)
(1870–1875)
Copper, 3.7 g, 15 mm

1 Pai - Sayaji Rao III
1944–1950 (1887–1893)
Copper, 2.1 g, 19 mm

THE COIN GALLERIES OF BARODA ◆ 45

Princely State of Baroda – Rupee
3 Pies = 1 Pice, 4 Pices = 1 Anna, 16 Annas = 1 Rupee

½ Paisa - Khande Rao
1275–1277 (1859–1861)
Copper, 3.4 g, 22 mm

½ Paisa - Sayaji Rao III
1937–1948 (1880–1891)
Copper, 7.8 g, 19 mm

1 Paisa - Satyaji Rao II
(Amreli mint)
(1819–1847)
Copper, 6.85 g, 19 mm

1 Paisa - Sayaji Rao II
1234–1248 (1819–1833)
Copper, 10.4 g, 21.0 mm

Princely State of Baroda – Rupee
3 Pies = 1 Pice, 4 Pices= 1 Anna, 16 Annas = 1 Rupee

1 Paisa - Sayaji Rao II
(1819 - 1847)
(1819–1847)
Copper, 10.1 g, 19 mm

1 Paisa - Sayaji Rao II
(AH1235–1264/
1819–1847AD)
1240–1241 (1825–1826)
Copper, 10.12 g, 19 mm

1 Paisa - Sayaji Rao II
1253–1255 (1838–1839)
Copper, 10 g, 20 mm

1 Paisa - Sayaji Rao II
1256–1263 (1840–1847)
Copper, 10.42 g, 21.6 mm

Princely State of Baroda – Rupee
3 Pies = 1 Pice, 4 Pices = 1 Anna, 16 Annas = 1 Rupee

1 Paisa - Sayaji Rao II
1256 (1840)
Copper, 7.6 g, 20 mm

1 Paisa - Sayaji Rao II
1260 (1844)
Copper, 10.24 g. 19 mm

1 Paisa - Akbar Shah II
[Ganpat Rao]
1264–1268 (1848–1852)
Copper, 8.26 g, 18.82 mm

1 Paisa - Kande Rao
(1856-)
Copper, 6.95 g, 20.88 mm

Princely State of Baroda – Rupee
3 Pies = 1 Pice, 4 Pices= 1 Anna, 16 Annas = 1 Rupee

1 Paisa - Khande Rao
1274 (1858)
Copper, 8.54 g, 19 mm

1 Paisa - Khande Rao
1274–1277 (1858–1861)
Copper, 6.98 g, 21 mm

1 Paisa - Khande Rao
1281–1285 (1865–1869)
Copper,.75 g, 19 mm

1 Paisa - Malhar Rao
1288–1290 (1870–1875)
Copper, 7.63 g, 20.5 mm

Princely State of Baroda – Rupee
3 Pies = 1 Pice, 4 Pices = 1 Anna, 16 Annas = 1 Rupee

1 Paisa - Malhar Rao
(1870–1875)
Copper, 7.75 g, 26 mm

1 Paisa - Sayaji Rao III
1940–1942 (1883–1885)
Copper, 7.58 g, 24 mm

1 Paisa - Sayaji Rao III
1941–1950 (1884–1893)
Copper, 6.7 g, 24.65 mm

1 Paisa - Sayaji Rao III
1949 (1892)
Copper, 8 g, 22 mm

Princely State of Baroda – Rupee
3 Pies = 1 Pice, 4 Pices= 1 Anna, 16 Annas = 1 Rupee

1 Paisa - Sayaji Rao III
(Baroda)
1311–1313 (1894–1896)
Copper, 7.5 g, 20 mm

2 Paisa - Malhar Rao
1288–1290 (1871–1873)
Copper, 16.1 g

2 Paisa - Sayaji Rao III
(Baroda)
1940–1950 (1883–1947)
Copper, 16.3 g, 29.5 mm

2 Annas - Sayaji Rao III
(1877–1881)
Silver, 1.4 g, 10 mm

Princely State of Baroda – Rupee
3 Pies = 1 Pice, 4 Pices= 1 Anna, 16 Annas = 1 Rupee

2 Annas - Sayaji Rao III
1949 (1892)
Silver, 1.4 g, 15.5 mm

2 Annas - Sayaji Rao III
1951–1952 (1894–1895)
Silver, 1.4 g, 14 mm

4 Annas - Sayaji Rao III
1292–1299 (1875–1882)
Silver, 2.8 g, 12 mm

4 Annas - Sayaji Rao III
1949 (1892)
Silver

Princely State of Baroda – Rupee
3 Pies = 1 Pice, 4 Pices = 1 Anna, 16 Annas = 1 Rupee

4 Annas - Sayaji Rao III
1951–1952 (1894–1895)
Silver

½ Rupee - Shah Alam II
[Anand Rao]
(1798–1806)
Silver, 5.80 g, 17.42 mm

½ Rupee - [Anand Rao]
1800
Silver, 5.86 g

½ Rupee - Anand Rao
(Ahmadabad mint)
(1806–1837)
Silver, 5.6 g, 18 mm

Princely State of Baroda – Rupee
3 Pies = 1 Pice, 4 Pices= 1 Anna, 16 Annas = 1 Rupee

½ Rupee - Muhammad Akbar II [Anand Rao]
1222–1234 (1807–1819)
Silver, 5.70 g, 18.40 mm

½ Rupee - Akbar Shah II [Sayaji Rao II]
1238–1262 (1823–1846)
Silver, 5.8 g, 16.2 mm

½ Rupee - Muhammad Akbar II [Ganpat Rao]
1264–1272 (1847–1856)
Silver, 5.65 g, 16.09 mm

½ Rupee - Muhammad Akbar II [Khande Rao]
1267–1282 (1851–1870)
Silver, 5.63 g, 16.78 mm

Princely State of Baroda – Rupee
3 Pies = 1 Pice, 4 Pices = 1 Anna, 16 Annas = 1 Rupee

½ Rupee - Khande Rao
(Baroda)
1274–1283 (1858–1867)
Silver, 5.8 g, 16 mm

½ Rupee - Malhār Rao
1287–1290 (1870–1873)
Silver, 5.8 g, 17.2 mm

½ Rupee - Sayaji Rao III
1292–1302 (1875–1885)
Silver, 5.8 g, 5 mm

½ Rupee - Sayaji Rao III
1948–1949 (1891–1892)
Silver

Princely State of Baroda – Rupee
3 Pies = 1 Pice, 4 Pices= 1 Anna, 16 Annas = 1 Rupee

½ Rupee - Sayaji Rao III
1951–1952 (1894–1895)
Silver

1 Rupee - Sayaji Rao III
1292–1302
Silver, 11 g, 20 mm

1 Rupee - Shah Alam II
(Sankheda Mint)
(1771–1818)
Silver, 11.34 g, 21.4 mm

1 Rupee - Anand Rao
(1788–1808)
Silver, 11.64 g, 22.22 mm

Princely State of Baroda – Rupee
3 Pies = 1 Pice, 4 Pices = 1 Anna, 16 Annas = 1 Rupee

1 Rupee - Shah Alam II
[Anand Rao] (Ankush mint)
(1788–1802)
Silver, 11.34 g, 21 mm

1 Rupee - Manaji Rao under
Shah Alam II
(1791–1792)
Silver, 11.6 g, 20 mm

1 Rupee - Anand Rao
1221–1235 (1806–1820)
Silver, 11.30 g, 22.0 mm

1 Rupee - Muhammad
Akbar II [Anand Rao]
(Ahmadabad mint)
1225–1233 (1810–1818)
Silver, 11.60 g, 22.30 mm

Princely State of Baroda – Rupee
3 Pies = 1 Pice, 4 Pices = 1 Anna, 16 Annas = 1 Rupee

1 Rupee - Satyaji Rao II
1237–1242 (1822–1827)
Silver, 11.4 g, 21 mm

1 Rupee - Sayaji Rao II
1244–1248 (1829–1833)
Silver, 11.40 g, 22.45 mm

1 Rupee - Satyaji Rao II
1247–1260 (1832–1844)
Silver, 11.5 g, 21 mm

1 Rupee - Muhammad Akbar II [Ganpat Rao]
1264–1272 (1848–1856)
Silver, 11.40 g, 19.60 mm

Princely State of Baroda – Rupee
3 Pies = 1 Pice, 4 Pices= 1 Anna, 16 Annas = 1 Rupee

1 Rupee - Khande Rao
1274–1287 (1858–1870)
Silver, 10.96 g, 20.60 mm

1 Rupee - Malhar Rao
1287–1293 (1870–1876)
Silver, 11.5 g, 19 mm

1 Rupee - Sayaji Rao III
1948–1949 (1891–1892)
Silver, 11.4 g, 30 mm

1 Rupee - Sayaji Rao III
1951–1956 (1894–1899)
Silver, 11.37 g, 28 mm

Princely State of Baroda – Rupee
3 Pies = 1 Pice, 4 Pices= 1 Anna, 16 Annas = 1 Rupee

⅙ Mohur - Sayaji Rao III
1951–1959 (1894–1902)
Gold, 1.18 g, 14.5 mm

⅓ Mohur - Sayaji Rao III
1942 (1885)
Gold, 2.39 g, 16 mm

⅓ Mohur - Sayaji Rao III
1959 (1902)
Gold, 2.39 g, 16 mm

1 Mohur - Sayaji Rao III
1945–1959 (1888–1902)
Gold, 21 mm

The coins of the early period of Baroda State need detailed study and research. So, one will have to go through the old records and research for documentation of coins minted at various mints and about mints which are yet unknown.

From the brief history of Gaekwads, it is very clear that there can be no coinage for Damajirao-I and Pilajirao as they were only Mutaliks in the army of Maratha king. Baroda was wrested from the Mughals around 1734 A.D. and around this period, Baroda State came into existence. So any coinage of Baroda has to be after this period only. The earliest dated coin, as stated above, was with the symbol of Scimitar, Sword and is in the name of Shah Alam II.

Govindrao's coin indicates the Persian letter 'GO' for Govinrao, Nagari, 'Ma' for Manaji, 'Aa' for Anandrao, and so on. Baroda Mint coins bear the symbol of sword, which is adopted as Damajirao-I was a valiant swordsman.

The various mints observed are:
i. Baroda Mint
ii. Petlad Mint
iii. Ahmedabad Mint
iv. Amreli Mint
v. Sankheda Mint
vi. Jambusar Mint

Baroda Mint coins usually bear the sword symbol, so do the coins minted at Sankheda and some coins of Petlad mint as well. Coins minted at the Amreli mint are observed from the reign of Sayajirao II and continue till the reign of Sayajirao III. Ahmedabad mint was one of the Maratha confederacy mints and bore the 'Ankush' symbol. Baroda States coins minted at Ahmedabad mint have an additional symbol 'GA' for Gaekwads. This mint was taken over by the British in 1835 A.D. and was closed down.

Jambusar mint coins have 'Mace' as the symbol and bear regnal year and mint name.

I. BARODA MINT:

Mughal rulers between AH 1174 and AH 1273
a. Shah Alam II AH 1174 to 1221/A.D. 1760–1806
b. M. Akbar II AH 1221 to 1253/A.D. 1806–1837
c. Bahadurshah II AH 1253 to 1273/A.D. 1837–1858

Coins In The Name Of

a. SHAH ALAM II: [AH 1174 to 1221 (47 years)]
Govindrao: AH 1182 to 1185
Sayajirao I: AH 1185 to 1192
Fateh Singh I: AH 1192 to 1204
Manajirao: AH 1204 to 1208
Govindrao: AH 1208 to 1215
Anadrao: AH 1215 to 1221

b. MUHAMMAD AKBAR II: [AH 1221 to 1253 (32 years)]
Anadrao: AH 1221 to 1235 (Regnal Year 1 to 14)
Sayajirao II: AH 1235 to 1264 (Regnal Years 15 to 44)
Note: Coins continued to be minted in the name of M. Akbar II even after his death and his regnal years continued.
Ganpatrao: AH 1264 to 1273 (Regnal years 43 to 52)
Khanderao: AH 1273 to 1287 (AH 1273 Regnal years 52 and 53)

Further Minting Of Coins:

Even after the collapse of the Mughal empire in AH 1273 the coins continued to be minted in Mughal pattern but without the name of the Mughal king and regnal years. Khanderao's coins continued with AH dates but with changes in sword direction as well as change in reverse design as

Khanderao was conferred with the title Commander of the Sovereign Band and this design even continued later on.

Malharrao: AH 1287 to 1292 – coins with AH dates

Sayajirao III: AH 1292to 1357/VS 1932 to 1995

AH 1302 recorded on Baroda Mint coins. Coins with VS dates observed from the year VS 1937 on copper coins and VS 1948 on silver coins.

Pratapsingh: VS 1995 to 2008/A.D. 1939–1995

Only Gold Mohras reported.

II. AMRELI MINT:

Only copper coins were minted at this mint. Till date silver coins are not reported. The coins were minted during the reigns of Sayajirao II, Ganpatrao, Khanderao and Sayajirao III. Coins were minted in Mughal pattern with AH dates; the last AH date observed is 1312. Different symbols are observed on these coins, the maximum being during Sayajirao II. On most of the coins, the symbol of the sword was observed.

III. PETLAD MINT:

Coins from this mint are observed during the reign of Ananadrao and are in the name of Shah Alam II. Regnal years 1 to 7 are reported. The design is like Baroda Mint except for the Nagari symbol, but sword is observed. Coins of later kings are not reported yet.

IV. SANKHEDA MINT:

Coins are like Baroda mints coins. Not many coins are available of this mint.

V. AHMEDABAD MINT:

Ahmedabad mint was a Maratha mint from A.D. 1757 to 1800. It was leased to Baroda from 1800 to 1804 A.D., returned in 1804, then released to Baroda in 1806 and ceded to Baroda in A.D. 1817. It was annexed by East India Company in A.D. 1818 and finally closed in A.D. 1835. It has **Ankush** as the symbol. For Baroda, an additional symbol of Gaekwad was depicted.

VI. JAMBUSAR COINS:

A regnal year and mint name are observed on these coins with MACE as the symbol. Gaekwad symbol is not observed.

6 HISTORICAL VISIT TO BARODA

Baroda is best known for its heritage and historical sites. Often described as the cultural capital of Gujarat, much of modern Baroda was shaped by Sayajirao III, a far-sighted ruler in the late 19th century who patronised art and music, introduced free primary education, and established institutions such as the Bank of Baroda, a railway system and the university. The city's beautiful old quarter is filled with heritage buildings, and the historical city of Champaner – a UNESCO World Heritage Site – located an hour's drive out of town, provide a fascinating insight into the past and will prove to be irresistible for history and culture buffs.

LAXMI VILAS PALACE

Laxmi Vilas Palace is one of the most majestic structures in India and was the private residence of Maharaja Sayajirao Gaekwad III. Known to be the largest private dwelling of the size equivalent to four times of the Buckingham Palace, this magnificent palace is a must-visit when in Vadodara. Sprawling across an area of about 700 acres, it is still home to the royal family of Vadodara, the Gaekwads. The lush gardens of the palace add to the beauty of the entire experience of being there. Lucky tourists can spot monkeys or peacocks strutting around. The grounds also include a

10-hole golf course. In earlier times, a small zoo was also a part of the area. What remains today is a small pond and a few crocodiles.

The striking palace was constructed in 1890 and took nearly twelve years to complete. The total cost of the construction was around £180,000. The chief architect of the palace was Major Charles Mant. He followed the Indo-Saracenic style while constructing the palace which is a hybrid of the Hindu, Gothic and Mughal architectural forms with the presence of domes, minarets and arches. It also incorporates several other buildings within its complex including the LVP Banquets and Conventions, Moti Baug Palace and the Maharaja Fateh Singh Museum building. An excellent audio tour with free drink and snack are included in the ticket price.

The museum building was mainly constructed as a school for the Maharaja's children. Today, the museum houses an extraordinary collection of paintings by Raja Ravi Verma and various other artefacts gathered from all around the world. A good blend of both foreign as well as local materials and workmanship was used in the construction of the palace. Red stone was brought in from Agra, blue trap stone from Poona, marbles from Rajasthan and Italy were used while twelve workmen from Venice laid down the beautiful montage floor of the Darbar Hall of the palace.

The planning of the building is totally on western patterns. Various palaces like Amber and Bikaner have only one entry with the public use areas being provided at the entry and the semi-public and private areas coming after that. In Laxmi Vilas Palace, Baroda separate entries have been provided to the Durbar kings residence and Zenana. It also contains a new breed of rooms like state dining billiards rooms etc. The building, which covers an area of 100,000 sq. feet, is laid out in a garden like a British country house.

The façade of the building has a great variety of treatment, the Durbar Hall on the left having Mughalized domes and chhatris, the Maharaja's residence having the Bharatpur influence and the Zenana having local Gujrat influence with more florid art. The parapet details are Rajput from Chittor. The sikharas that have been used are a Hindu influence. The tower has a British influence and was originally conceived as a clock tower. The circular ventilators have their roots in the church architecture. Mughal cusped arches have been used. They are full of various arches. Mughal chajjas have also been used, ELEVATION –FAÇADE. The arch as such gives the feeling of a Venelian arch. It is just a modified form of a ventiar arch. The sikharas that have been used in the façade without knowing its significance in Zenana are totally irrelevant as a Sikhara is never used in secular buildings. Mant rejected from the start any idea of a dry symmetrical pattern and allowed the styles to melt into one another. The exterior of the Maharaja's apartments was dressed up in the garb of Hindu martial architecture, with most of the detail borrowed from the fortress of Bharatpur. The public apartments, however, moved more into a Moghul style, while the ladies' quarters ended in a forest of domes and canopies copied from the Jain temples of Gujarat. Likewise, the materials used were a blend of East and West. The basic construction was brick faced with red sandstone from the quarries of Agra, with some blue trap stone from Poona and marble from the quarries of Rajasthan. Workmen from Madras came to apply the 'chunam' plaster to many of the interior walls. Then twelve workmen from the Murano Company of Venice spent eighteen months in Baroda laying the floor of Venetian mosaic in the Durbar Hall. Carara marble was imported for the doorways of the hall, the pillars and the ornamental staircase. Mr. Tree from London made the moulding and gilding on the walls and ceilings. Period furniture, Old Masters and Venetian chandeliers completed the effect.

SAYAJI GARDENS

Sayaji Gardens, as the name suggests, is dedicated to Maharaja Sayajirao Gaekwad III by Maharaja Sayajirao Gaekwad III himself. It is the largest garden in the western region of India with a sprawling 45 hectares of land.

This was built in the year 1879 on the river Vishwamitri, and it comprises of a large spectrum of flora, with more than 99 species of trees to its name. That's not all. This park also houses two museums, a planetarium, a zoo, a toy train for children and a flower clock. So many utilities under one roof, make this attraction the most sought after in the State of Gujarat. Constructed by the Gaekwads in 1894, the Vadodara Museum and Picture Gallery is host to umpteen numbers of relics relating to a wide range of fields right from archaeology to geology. The main attractions being the skeleton of the gigantic blue whale. The Floral Clock is a huge structure in the park which is a one-of-a-kind constructions in the State. The mechanism of the clock is very minutely designed to ensure that the time given by the clock is accurate. The Sayaji Baug Zoo has a rich collection of fauna featuring 167 types of 1103 animals. Recently, an aquarium containing 45 species of fish was added to the SayajiBaug Zoo. The Sardar Patel Planetarium, situated near the main entrance of the Sayaji Gardens, offers daily public shows as well as special shows to educational universities. There are three entrance gates. The main gate is at Sayaji square (informally known as "Kala Ghoda Chowk" or "black horse square" because of an equestrian statue standing there). This gate is only 800 metres from the main city railway station and even less from the city bus stand. The third gate is at Rana Pratap square in Fatehganj area, and the second gate stands somewhere in between the first and third gates.

It is also known as "Kamati Baug". It is the biggest garden in Western India with an estimated area of over 100 acres. It has one of the biggest floral clocks in India and in the world.

FLORAL CLOCK

The floral clock was the first of its kind in the State. It consists of an hour, minute and seconds hand that move on the 20 ft (6.1 m) diameter dial. The machinery moving the clock is underground, giving the clock a natural look.

VADODARA MUSEUM

Constructed by the Gaekwads in 1894, the Vadodara Museum and Picture Gallery is host to umpteen numbers of relics relating to a wide spectrum of fields right from archaeology to geology.

It also houses a few rare personal collection pieces of Maharaja Sayajirao III. Most noteworthy relics are the 109 miniature paintings from the Mughal times, a Persian version of Mahabharata specially commissioned by Mughal Emperor Akbar and 11th century Shiva Natraj among others.

SARDAR PATEL PLANETARIUM

The planetarium is situated near the main gate of Sayaji Baug. It is a pyramid-shaped building having capacity of 200 spectators. It conducts daily public shows as well as special shows for educational institutions. The shows are available in Hindi, English and Gujarati. The planetarium also gives you information about a variety of planets and stars.

TOY TRAIN/JOY TRAIN

The toy train ride runs on a track which is 10 inches (250 mm) wide covering a distance of 3.5 km and offering the view of the entire garden to riders. The ride was a gift to the children of Vadodara from the royal Gaekwad dynasty.

Now a new train has been introduced instead of this small toy train. Its name is Joy train in which even adults can sit. Joy train is slightly bigger than the toy train. A new platform "Swami Vivekananda Station" is created for this train. The train timings are from 10 A.M. to 10 P.M., and it is closed on Thursdays. During the full journey of about 20 minutes the people are informed about the heritage of Vadodara and Kamatibag (Garden) through speakers in the train.

The video for the popular song "Chakke pe Chakka, Chakke pe Gadi…" by Shankar Jaikishan from the film Brahmachari was shot on this train.

THE ZOO AND AQUARIUM

The Sayaji Baug Zoo is situated on both the banks of the Vishwamitri river. In Sayajibaug the zoo was opened as part of the original park in 1879. The zoo offers 167 types of 1103 animals of various species. Asiatic lions are the most popular attractions. It also has a different bird zoo which has many different types of birds.

An aquarium was added to the zoo in 1962. It contains 45 species of fishes.

CHAMPANER-PAVAGADH ARCHAEOLOGICAL PARK

Being included in the elite list of the World Heritage Sites across the globe, this marvellous archaeological park set in the heart of the city of Champaner and amidst the Pavagadh hills is one of the most sought-after places in Gujarat. Though it is not located in proper Baroda, it is included in the heritage list of Baroda. It is located near Baroda.

Why wouldn't it be as it is withholding a lot of historical as well as mythological significance. The Park comprises of umpteen number of splendid architectural wonders consisting of both Hindu & Islamic styles of design. Not only this, an interesting piece of trivia regarding this place is that the hill of Pavagadh is believed to be a chunk of the Himalayas that was originally carried by Hanuman to Lanka in the Ramayana epic. With such a rich history to its name, this makes up for a really intriguing place to visit.

EME TEMPLE

EME seems to be a strange name for a temple. It stands for Electrical and Mechanical Corps, in honour of the people who built the temple. A symbol of the secularity practised in the Indian Army, the EME Temple in Vadodara is an aluminium-clad abode, constructed at the intersection of the ancient and modern period. Also known as the Dakshinamurthy temple, it primarily houses a massive idol of Lord Shiva, along with a miniature Lord

Ganesha (specially brought in from Mahabalipuram). There is also a silver arch with the holy words "Om Namah Shivaya" engraved on it.

It is a popular opinion among archaeologists that this temple is unique in its design, concept and geodesic design covered with war scraps and aluminium sheets. The unique aspect is how the temple supports secularism by incorporating holy symbols from every religion in its structure. The Kalash on the top symbolises Hinduism. The Dome signifies Islam. The Tower represents Christianity. The Golden structure above the tower expresses Buddhism. The Entrance stands for Jainism.

The Indian Army brings together a diverse set of people from all over the nation, each with their culture, traditions and religions. Since it would be difficult to accommodate all kinds of places of worship for the varied faiths that these people adhere to, it was thought to build a structure that integrates a relic from every dominant religion of India. In 1966, an EME Corp initiated this idea in the army quarters of Vadodara, which led to the construction of a one-of-a-kind sacred abode in the history of the world, where people of any faith could come together under one roof. This is the beauty and speciality of the EME Temple, located in the western state of Gujarat. It should form a crucial part of your itinerary if you are in Vadodara and want a place to unwind or feel spiritual upliftment.

KHANDERAO MARKET

It pretty much seemed like Maharaja Sayajirao Gaekwad III, just needed a random reason to build an edifice. The Khanderao Market is an extravagant building built under his supervision in 1906 and was a gift to the municipality on the completion of 25 years of his authoritative administration.

He dedicated this building to Maharaja Khanderao Gaekwad, and it is now a haven to several offices, counting the Vadodara Municipal Corporation as well.

The palatial building named after Maharaja Khanderao Gaekwad was built in 1906 by Maharaja Sayajirao Gaekwad III. On completing 25 years of his administration, Sayajirao gave this building as a gift to the municipality of Vadodara. Today it houses several offices including the city municipal corporation and on the backside of the building is a vegetable market.

MAKARPURA PALACE

Makarpura Palace was initially constructed with the motive of serving as a summer palace for the royal family of the Gaekwads.

Built in 1870 and given an Italian touch of architecture, it was renovated years after it was built because the palace was left unused as the royal family preferred spending most of their summers in the relatively cooler Nilgiris of Tamil Nadu. It now serves as a training school called No.17 Tetra School used by the Indian Air Force.

AUROBINDO ASHRAM

The Aurobindo Ashram, also known as Arvind Ashram or AuroNivas, is the ashram that was the dwelling place of Aurobindo Ghosh during his stay in Baroda in the years 1894 to 1906. Located at Dandia Bazar in the city of Vadodara in Gujarat, this was the first-ever ashram to gain immense popularity and respect in the southern areas of the State.

The Aurobindo Ashram, which contains 23 rooms in all, houses a library, a study room and a sales emporium. Relics of Sri Aurobindo and all rare books that have been written by or about him can also be found here. The ashram is open to any and every person who is interested in meditation, spirituality or The Mother. The Mother, who was originally known as Mirra Alfassa, was a disciple and collaborator of Sri Aurobindo. Shri Aurobindo believed her to be the incarnation of Mother Divine and hence named her The Mother. The Arvind Ashram serves as a national memorial which was visited by many prominent personalities during those times. The peace prevailing in the meditation halls and the campus, in general, is appreciated by the visitors.

MAHARAJA SAYAJIRAO UNIVERSITY

The Maharaja Sayajirao University is a premium institution in the city of Vadodara, in Gujarat. The University has evolved from the Baroda College (1881) which was one of the oldest and most respected centres of education in Western India. It was later renamed after its benefactor Maharaja Sayajirao Gaekwad III, the former ruler of Baroda State. The present Maharaja Sayaji Rao University has lived up to the name of its predecessor and done justice to the great Gaekwad dynasty to whom it owes its existence. Apart from being an educational institution, it is also a heritage site. Originally established as a college in 1881, it became a university in 1949 after the independence of the country. It was later renamed after its benefactor Maharaja Sayajirao Gaekwad III, the former ruler of Baroda State belonging to the royal Gaekwad dynasty of the Marathas.

The university is built upon 275 acres of land and boasts of 14 faculties including arts, commerce, education and psychology, family and community sciences, fine arts, journalism and communication, law, management studies, medicine, performing arts, science, social work, technology and engineering, and pharmacy. The Institution has become a paragon in the field of education with 90 departments, 3 constitutional colleges and several other centres which provide education at varying levels starting from kindergarten to PhD. It is also spreading its wings towards more modern subjects like fashion designing, catering technology and hotel management to keep pace with the times.

Originally known as the Baroda College of Science, it became a university in 1949 after the independence of the country. It is a teaching and residential university and the only university in Gujarat that has

English as the medium of instruction for all courses. Currently, more than 1200 well-qualified staff members and 1500 administrative staff and more than 35000 students have created a whole new world of learning inside the historical campus of Maharaja Sayaji Rao University. All-in-all, the Maharaja Sayaji Rao University is a well-established learning centre where students get ready for the modern world in the very lap of a great historical heritage.

KIRTI MANDIR, VADODARA

Maharaja Sayajirao Gaekwad III was so powerful and affluent that he had an entire monument built to commemorate the cremation of his family members. This monument was called the Kirti Mandir.

Widely known as the Temple of Fame, this structure was also constructed to celebrate the fifty years of his mighty administration. One of the carvings on the cenotaph makes one reminisce about the good old days, during which India was not divided into so many states and territories, due credit to the undivided map of India displayed on the central arch. The 33 m high central arch is also ornamented with the sun, the moon and the earth and the rooms behold the sculptures and photographs of the members of the Gaekwad family. The sun, the moon and the earth in bronze with the undivided map of India adorn the shikhara of Kirti Mandir. It was built in 1936 as part of the Diamond Jubilee celebrations of Maharaja Sayajirao Gaekwad III. The temple houses five wall paintings by artist Raja Ravi Varma showing various phases of the battle of Mahabharata.

It is believed that Sayajirao Maharaja built this Kirti Mandir in the memory of deceased members of the royal Gaekwad family and the edifice is dedicated to Lord Mahadev. Today it is a major tourist attraction in the city. The outstanding stone building is constructed in the shape of a letter "E" with terraces, balconies, domes and a central shikhara that rises to approximately 35 metres. The interiors of the Kirti Mandir are marble treated and brilliantly decorated with intricately carved murals. The walls of the central hall are adorned with many impressive murals such as the Gangavataran, Life of Meera, battle of Mahabharat and NatirPoojan which are all very well-preserved works from the renowned Bengali artist Nandalal Bose. Statues, as well as precious photographs of eminent members of the Gaekwad family, are also displayed for public viewing.

According to annals of history, the golden era in the Maratha rule of Baroda commenced when Sayajirao Maharaja came into power in 1875. He is well remembered by people even today for his work to establish necessary primary education, a university, a library system, tile factories and model textile and thereby modernise Baroda, which resulted in building the image of Baroda as a modern industrial hub. In addition to the Kirti Mandir, Vadodara has a number of diverse attractions such as palaces, buildings, monuments, gardens, museums as well as modern entertainment.

For the tourists, there are endless possibilities to indulge in sightseeing, though the town is lesser-known compared to other major tourist attractions in India. Vadodara's one of the tourist attraction is Kirti Mandir situated on the north of the statue of Prince Fatehsinhrao Gaekwad near the Vishwamitri Bridge. With a cluster of Shiva temples it was built to commemorate the cremation of the members of the Gaekwad family. This "E" shaped large magnificent stone building with domes, terraces, balconies and central shikhara rising to about 33 metres. According to Sayajirao Gaekwad, it was built to commemorate the benefactors of his state irrespective of their race, caste or creed.

The Kirti Mandir of Baroda was built with a cost of Rs.50,000. It preserves the statues and photographs of the members of the royal family in its various rooms. The interior of this elegant structure is marble finished and on the walls of the central hall are the murals Gangavataran, battle of Mahabharat, Life of Meera and Natir Pooja-executed by the famous Bengali artist Nandalal Bose.

SURSAGAR LAKE

Sur Sagar lake, also known as the Chand Talao is a lake situated in the middle of the city of Vadodara in the State of Gujarat in India. The lake was rebuilt with stone masonry in the 18th Century. The water in this lake remains in it for the whole year. A concrete wall surrounds the lake on which the people sit. A 120 ft tall statue of Lord Shiva built by Vadodara Mahanagar Seva Sadan stands in the middle of the lake. There are many underwater gates in the lake which empty the lake if it overflows. The water from the lake empties in the Vishvamitra River. The lake is used for boating. The statue of Lord Shiva is lit with lights on Mahashivratri.

Decked with lush greenery on all sides, Sursagar lake is an example of exemplary architecture and mesmerising beauty. Enjoy paddle-boating in these jade waters and go around the majestic 120-foot statue of Lord Shiva that looks upon the lake. Relaxing on the boundary wall under the starry night is a great way to get away from the monotonous, fast-paced city lives.

As of 2015, boating has been prohibited in the lake due to various issues.

The lake is known for a large number of suicides which occur yearly. Between January and October 2014, 15 suicides were reported to the authorities, who attribute the lake's isolation and seclusion to its choice destination for suicides.

NAZARBAUGH PALACE

Nazarbaug Palace or NazarBāgh Palace was the Gaekwad's royal palace in the city of Vadodara, Gujarat state, Western India. The NazarBāgh Palace' was built in 1721. It had three storeys and is the oldest palace in Baroda. It was constructed by Malhār Rao Gaekwad in the late 19th century. This palace was used on ceremonial occasions by the Gaekwads. Till recently, it housed the royal family heirlooms. It had solid gold and silver guns, each barrel weighing over 100 kg. The grounds also contain the Shīsh Mahal, a Palace of Glass.

The Palace had a classic look, so in Gujarati, it was told about its look as 'Nazarnalaage' from which it was named Nazar. The Palace also had a beautiful garden from which its name included baug. So, it was named as Nazarbaug Palace.

The white-stucco palace was the depository of the jewels of the Gaekwad family, and in 1927 the collection was believed to be worth $10,000,000 at the time, including a diamond necklace which carried both the Star of the South diamond, weighing around 125 carats, and the English Dresden; another important part of the collection was a cloth embroidered with precious stones and seed pearls, made to cover the tomb of Muhammad.

The palace was in a state of ruin and did not reflect its former glory. The inside was ripped out after an alleged robbery. The grounds were used as a car park. Visitors were allowed to walk around but not allowed to take photos. Such is the state of this once beautiful palace the root of Gaekwad rule in Vadodara that was unrecognisable and possibly the land will be sold off for apartment constructions.

In October 2014, the palace was completely razed with only rubble, and some parts of the floor remained. The collection also includes Indian Paintings, Graeco-Roman exhibits, Chinese and Japanese art. Once used on ceremonial occasions by the Gaekwads, this palace houses a Sheesh Mahal.

TOMB OF QUTUBUDDIN MUHAMMAD KHAN (HAZIRA MAQBARA)

The mausoleum (also known as Hazira Maqbara) contains the graves of Qutubuddin Muhammad Khan who was the tutor of Salim, son and successor of Akbar, and also that of his son Naurang Khan who held important offices in Gujarat under Akbar. Qutubuddin was the uncle of Mirza Aziz Koka, foster brother of Akbar and Governor of Gujarat thrice between 1573 A.D. and 1583 A.D. He was killed in 1583 by Muzaffar III, the last Sultan of Gujarat. Qutubuddin was a famed General in the army of Akbar, and he later became the Governor of the Baroda region.

Built on a high octagonal platform with small gaps facing cardinal directions, and with five arches on each side, the mausoleum resembles Humayun's mausoleum in Delhi. According to the Archaeological Survey of India (ASI), the mausoleum was built around 1586.

The mausoleum is located about 1 Km from the Pratapnagar railway overbridge.

TAMBEKARWADA

Tambekar Wada is located at Tambkear no Khancho, Raopura Area, Vadodara (Baroda). It is a three-storeyed building which is a typical Maratha Mansion, which was once the residence of BhauTambekar. Inside of Wada, there are some of the most beautiful but decaying 19th Century murals. The building is almost 140+ Years Old.

Tambekar Wada is a spacious, four-storey building that had been constructed in an oblong fashion. It is originally the former residence of the Baroda State Diwan or Minister, BhauTambekar, who owned the responsibility of the administration of the state. The walls, doors and ceilings on the first and second floors of this old fashion building are adorned with the best specimens of mural paintings dating back to the 17th and 18th centuries. Other wall paintings dating back to the first half of the 19th century represent epic scenes depicting the life of the people. The paintings are in polychrome and are of Maratha style of paintings of 19th century A.D. They are the best specimen of mural paintings in Gujarat. Most of the paintings have been restored by the Archaeological Survey of India. The ASI still attend to the chemical treatments of these paintings on a regular basis.

There are paintings of Lord Krishna in childhood breaking pot, Lord Krishna doing Raas with Gopis, Lord Ganesha in childhood etc. Also, it has British-Maratha fight paintings.

According to ASI, paintings in Tambekar Wada are made during the year 1874. There are ~300 Paintings in Wada from 1st to 3rd floor. The paintings are not only painted on walls, but also it is painted on door frames. Also, there is nice design of Jali's and wood carving. The backside of the building is in dilapidated condition. ASI & VMC plans to repair it.

THE WALLED CITY

The old city of Baroda is overcrowded, cluttered and extremely busy. That is how it has been for centuries. Drive into Mandvi – the city's vortex, and you will feel transported into medieval bazaars, shrines, glorious buildings, pols, wadas and padas. This is the old, heart of modern Baroda, once walled within 4 gates – Lehripuradarwaza, Pani Gate, Gendi Gate and ChampanerDarwaza.

The city once had a square foot called Killa-e-Daulatbad. Later, the four gates were added, all equidistant from Mandvi. Mandvi is at the centre of the walled city where the roads leading to the four gates intersect.

Life within the once walled area is vibrant and has a quint cultural mix. The wedding procession of Lord Narsinhji is one of the rituals which keeps traditions alive.

1. Laheripura Darwaza

This gate on the western side was the main entrance to the walled city. It was constructed along with other gates to build a fortified town in A.D. 1511 by the son and successor pf Mehmud Begada – Prince Khalikhan. The Gaekwad renovated the gate in the Maratha Rajput style in the 19th Century. It has three arches with images of Lord Ganesh and Goddess Durga. The central arch has a 'chhatri' and 'jharokha' where shehnai artists used to perform. Originally coppersmiths who were also known as 'laheris' lived near this gate.

2. Panigate

About 500 metres from Mandvi, Panigate served as the eastern gate to the walled city. Since the town was receiving water supply from the Raje and

Ajab lakes situated on the eastern side, this gate was called Pani (water) gate. The gate has four 10 feet wide arches in the Islamic style. A portion of the gate had collapsed and was restored a few years back. On its outer side, above the main arch, is a structure shaped like a lopsided triangle, similar to the human nose. It is popularly known as 'Baroda nu Naak' – a metaphor for the city's honour.

3. Gendi Gate

The southern gate is an Islamic style structure with four ribbed arches. A sloping roof was later constructed during the Maratha period. Rhinos, 'Gendas' in Gujarati, were kept near this gate. Gendi gate has also been referred to in old documents as 'Baranpura' locality in the walled city. Or it was in the direction of Burhanpur in Madhya Pradesh, much akin to the Baranpuri Bhagol in Surat which points to Burhanpur.

4. Champaner Darwaza

This gate faces northwards to Champaner and was constructed after the Champaner fort was captured by Mehmud Begada. It was strategically important for the Sultans to protect the capital of Gujarat Sultanate – Champaner – from any attack. Today, Champaner is the only UNESCO recognised World Heritage Site in Gujarat.

7 SOME UNKNOWN FACTS

Looking at the history before 1500 years regarding existence of Vadodara, it can be seen that today's Salatwada was the area known for some famous 'Salats'. They were living there, and each house was surrounded by Wada. That wada was echoing by the sounds of stone lead. There was an article written on Tamrpatra found while digging wada of Venirambhai. In the article about Tamrapatra, it is cited that there was village named Vatpatrak situated at the banks of river Vishawamitri (created by the Maharshi Vishwamitri) which was donated to the Brahmin named Bhanu.

Chandanavati of 11th Century was situated between the four gates of today's Baroda and the Vatpatrak village was situated at the banks of river Vishawamitri from Akota to Kamnath Mahadev of today's Baroda. Vatpatrak was originally shaped of 'Chausar – traditional Indian game'. Looking from the Mandavi, Baroda looked very attractive with 12 Paras and 15 lakes. There was the gate of Bawaman in the South-east direction. It is mentioned that Damajirao II built the Mandvi building in the year 1733. Sultan Muzafarshah II built the walls around the Baroda in the year 1511 and named it 'Dolatabad'.

There was betel plants garden behind today's Nagarwada area of Baroda which was expanded till the riverbank. The 'Stairwell (Vav)' situated besides Rajmahel is known as 'NavlakhiVav' due to the expenses incurred behind it, i.e. 9 Lacs gold coins. It was built by Suryaraj Kalchuri in the sixth - seventh century.

The area of Chandanvati between four gates and Dolatabad shaped as Baroda. There was a pit at the outskirts of old Baroda which was filled with water only in monsoon. Its water was used by the people of Baroda. The dried Chandan lake was observed by hardworking Sureshwar Desai, and the 'SURSAGAR LAKE' was created.

Mama's Pole: in the regime of the Sayajirao II (1818–1847), today's Raopura area was known as 'Sadashiv Peth'. There was mama's pole situated in Raopura surrounded by strong walls on both sides and a big gate. Its real name was Balchand Patel's Pole. Balchand Patel lived in this pole with the people, and his nephew did security job. His mama becomes mama of all people and known as mama's pole. There is also Jain derasar in the pole.

Hathila Hanuman: it's a tale dating back to 300 years ago. There is an area of Miya Mohammed's wadi in the South-east of today's Baroda, and there is an old Hanuman Temple at the border of Wadi. The name of this pole was "ShuraShalvini pole". This area was far away from the main village. The Shalvi community lived therein and did handloom work. One night the Vanzaera community came and ask for the shelter to one dignitary person named Shura of Shalvi community. The Vanzara community had brought an idol of Hanumanji, and they intended to build temple of him. The second day when the entire Vanzara community wished to move on, the cart having the Hanumanji idol became immovable. In spite of many efforts, the people were unable to move the cart which has the idol of Hanumanji. Later on, the temple was made on that place, and therefore, it was known as Hathila Hanuman.

Dala Patel: Dala Patel's Pole is situated among Narsinhji's Pole located between Laheripura and Mandvi. Before the 12th century, there was a village named 'Tankanpur' instead of Padra. The Takanpur name changed later on, and it became Padmavati from the name of the mother. Today's Padra is situated between this Tankanpur and Padmavati. Dala Patel was origin of Piplav village of Ashapuri and moved to try his luck. He got the company of Vanzara community in the way. When Vanzara community stayed for one night in Baroda, Dala Patel was awake the entire night and decided to populate a village at the border of the village. In the next morning when the Vanzara community moved on, Dala Patel just stayed over there. He became Patel of Padra.

Chhotiya'shajiro: In Gujarat, there was the regime of Sultan Bahadurshah from 1526 to 1537. Today's Piramitar road was known as "Part of Nilkantheshwar Mahadev". There was one fakir named PirAmisha Taher. His monument exists today also. Piramitar area was known from his name. The lady named Chhotibibi was acting as dancer in the court of King Sayajirao II. With the passage of time, she made Hajiro, and after building Hajiro she went for Hajj to Khambhat where she died due to illness. This Chhotiya's Hajiro still exists in Piramitar.

Bhadhra Wadi Rangmahel: The History of Bhadhra Kacheri Building is not found yet, but it is believed that it has to be built for the residence of Kings. Miya Mohammed and his wife were leaving with very pageantry and joviality (rangorag). This might be the reason why it is known as Rangmahel. Miya Mohammed had hidden all his money in the nearby lake due to fear of Mohammed Begda and hid in Hajira made by him.

Madan of Madanzanpa: There was a criminal named Sherkhan Bali during 17th Century in Vadodara. Inam Mahendi was his companion. There was prostitute name MADAN. Due to InamMahendi, she becomes favourite prostitute of Sherkhan. She wished to build house with pond and temple of Mahadev near bank of pond in today Madanzanpa area. She dreamt of becoming Begam of Sherkhan. The pond also is known as 'Madan nu talav'. Once Inam Mehndi brought a girl for Sherkhan, but she made suicide into the pond. That girl was daughter of Dala Patel. Though regime of Sherkhan came to an end the area is known as Madanzanpa.

Sureshwar Desai: There were 2 Gujaratis who helped in the foundation of the Gaekwad Empire – Sureshwar Desai and Dala Patel. At the time of Desai King, Chandan Talav was only pit and shaped as lake. Desaigiri came into the hands of Sureshwar Desai. He bought Chandan lake area and built beautiful lake which was known as Sursagar. There were poor people residing around the haveli of Sureshwar Desai. The poor people were grinding mill for their survival. Due to this mill business, the whole area is known as Ghantipada.

Mard Pratap: Pratapsingh, basically, belonged to Rajasthan and was doing the job under Sherkhanbali in Baroda. He had his own soldiers. He made his residence besides Laheripura Darwaza and started work of distributing posts through Dromedary (sandhni). This work was beloved to be of courage and bravery. Therefore, he was renamed as 'Pratap Marda' and the pole where he resided known as 'Pratap Madghani pole'.

Ladbibi: There are 2 areas in between Mandvi to Gendigate way – 1) Moghalwado – Moghal soldiers were leaving with Moghal police and 2) Laadwado. Baroda was under the ruling of Sherkhan, and his cousin was Laadbibi. Laadbibi was married to Nawab of Patan, but she left her husband and lived in Baroda. She was wealthy lady, and her wealth was managed by Sureshwar Desai. Laadbibi liked one carpenter. That carpenter insulted a lady who belonged to family of Sureshwar Desai. Laadbibi died but the area known as Ladwado.

Kedareshwar: Damajirao II ruled Baroda from 1732 to 1769. He gave new face and new shape to the Mandvi. There were 8 queens out of which Damajirao II married solemnise with 6 queens. He was having differences with Peshwa. Peshwa restrains Damajirao II fraudulently. Thereafter his cousin brother Kedarjirao Gaekwad ruled. Kedarjirao Gaekwad founded Kedareshwar temple in Kirtimandir.

Wall picture: It is a tale before 1768. Goddess Lakshmi blessed Gopal Tambekar who lived in Tambe village, Dist. Satara. Gopal became a lender of money. He was also lending to Peshwas. Sayajirao had been honoured with the umpire after the death of Damajirao. Gopal Tambekar became vizier of Baroda. He built a big palace and was known as Tambekar's Wado. It is very famous due to its wall pictures which states story of that time.

Fatehpura: The ruling period of Fatehsinhrao II was 1800 to 1818. The building in which there is a school outside the Champaner gate was the residence of Fatehsinhrao II and that area is known as Fatehpura.

Gadiyali Pole: During the ruling of Fatehsinhrao, his residence was in Gadiyali Pole. To keep time, a watch was placed in the palace. Securities were ringing bell according to watch-Gadiyal and therefore the area known as Gadiyali Pole. Mint was also established in the palace.

Shastri's Pole: Shastri's pole is situated between Raopura and Anandpura. Anadpura was established in the name of Anandrao Gaekwad who ruled from 1800 to 1819. His vizier was Gangadhar Shastri Patvardhan. During that time, there were differences between Gaekwad and Peshwas. Kandojiroa, a cousin of Anandrao, made conspiracies to harm Anandrao. Kandojirao took the support of outside soldiers to besiege Shastri. But Shahstri came to know this and Kandojirao was caught and sent to Madras.

Kandojirao was very angry with Shastri. Shastri went Puna to solve the differences between Peshwa and Gaekwad. He was taking care of the interests of Gaekwads. He never came in in front of Peshwas. The enemies planned to finish Shastri. Peshwa invitees Shastri in temple function, and Shastri accepted and visited. Late at night, when Shastri was returning with his team, he was killed. He gave responsibility to Mairad, his honest team member, for his family but the pole is known as Shastri's pole.

Anusatini Tekri: Govindrao, a cousin of Anandrao, was planning to have the empire with the support of Peshwa. Mairad's soldiers and family of Shastri were opposite to each other. One day Mairad very carefully and actively sent Shastri's family to Baroda with his very honest man. Fatehsinhrao welcomed Shastri's family. He himself took care of Shastri's family. Shastri's son was appointed as vizier at the age of 20 years. Shastri's daughter became widow at an early age, and that was shocking to the public. She made an announcement that she wanted to be SATI after her husband. She was firm with her decision and became SATI in her residence which was just behind the Shastri's pole. The place was known as AnusatiniTekri.

Raopura – Bavajipura: Sayajirao II ruled after Anandrao. Vizier RavjiAyaji, from whose name Raopura area was named as Raopura, had made fix viziership of his future generation with the help of Britishers. After him, his son Sitaram became vizier whose name is remembered in the area Sitaram Wado. Sitaram did not have management skill, and therefore he called his uncle named BabajiAyaji – in whose name Bavajipura area is known. Bavajipura area was known as Nilkanthpura, and today also Nilkantheshwar Mahadev temple is situated in this area. At the south of this temple, Elephant was kept by Babaji and lateron this arear known as HATHIPOLE. There is one more area named DANDITABAZAR within this Bavajipura. There too many stories behind the name:

- A person who makes an important announcement with Dandi was known as crier – Dandi pitnar. It is possible that due to crier families, the area was known as Dandiya Bazar.
- Movement of life necessity things was made in carvan. Vanzaras of carvans were moving village to village and buys and sells by staying at one place. The place where Santhiyas of carvan gets to gather might be known as Santhiyabazar and later on known as dandiyabazar.
- To measure grain or other, use of Dandi, i.e. scale degree was very famous. The place where Dandi made might be known as Dandiya bazaar.
- Five-meterSadi was known as Dandye in Marathi. It might be possible that there might be a business of Dandye and therefore, area became famous as Dandiyabazar.

Suryamandir: In the time of vizier Ravji Ayaji, sun temple was built. RavjiAyaji went to Kashi where he met Pandit's daughter. They liked each other. In those days to keep more than one wife was fashion. With the passage of time, the Pandit daughter lost interest in society, and she asks for permission to build Sun temple. RavjiAyaji was surprised by this demand. The Pandit daughter made him understand that "A lady always needs company of a man and you are always busy with your kingdom and your work, and if you get time, you are busy with your wife and children. In society, the second wife never gets respect as the first wife, mother or sister gets. You are my son, but far away…" RavjiAyaji gave permission to build temple, and the temple was built. But looking at the temple Pandit's daughter told that face of sun idol is at east. If idol's eyesite will be on nagar, then it will be demolished. Shastris gave solution to this to put hathi – elephant in front of idol. RavjiAyaji thought about the timing of preparation of statue of Hathi. One of his kingdom members told that there is idol of hathi at the Anusati's Tekri which can be placed here. The labours placed the idol and completed the temple.

Kutubuddin no Hajiro: In India, the outside Muslims always tried to demolish Hindu art, but Mughals are different. They tried to decorate India as their own country. King Akbar won Gujarat from Humayu. Kutubuddin's Hajiro was building since time of Akbar. It is situated at the south of Baroda on the way to Makarpura. In year 1575, Akbar has appointed Mirza Aziz, son of his stepmother, as administrator. This Mirza Aziz appointed his uncle Kutubuddin as Manager of Baroda. Either Akbar made this Hajiro or Kutubuddin himself made this Hajiro for his rest. Kutubuddin was killed in 1585, and his dead body was buried in this Hajiro. There is tomb of Kutubuddin in Hajira. This Hajiro was built above the land around at 12-foot height. It was tale that there is underground space under this Hajira and there is way to go Pavagadh from this underground. There is beautiful artistic work in the building.

Bhutiyowado: Though today's generation does not believe in Ghost – Bhut and all but there is some evidence. In year 1847, Ganpatrao Gaekwad handled the seat at the age of 20 years. On the way from Mandvi to Champanerdarwaza, there was green bungalow – Palace of that time. There was Mehta pole besides it. Shah Saudagarlallu Mehta was residing in that Mehta pole. There was Goverdhannath temple at the right side in the pole. This place is known as bhutiyawada till 1947. The owner of that bhutiyawada was Vitthalrao Risalghar. He died at very young age, but due to his lusting nature, his soul did not get rest in peace. He had lot of money, and too much money was in the underground place. His soul was attached to his money, and some people came to know about this, so they went away from the bhutiyawada.

One-time Maharaj Govinglalji entered in Baroda. There was confusion about his residence. Ganpatrao had decided to make him stay at bhutiyawada. Vaishanav became sad, but Maharaj made them agree to by saying that bhut will run away after his footprints. Magharajshree and his team entered in bhutiyawada. The team got scared due to different noises and came to bedroom of Maharaj. Maharaj understood and told them to sleep peacefully. Nothing happened in that wada the entire night. The second day it became talk of the town that Maharaj controlled bhut. Ganpatrao challenged Maharaj, "I can believe only if I see." Maharajshree accepted the challenge. At the second midnight, Govindrao sat beside Maharaj, and he saw one handsome man in front of Maharaj Shree. Maharaj identified him as Vitthalrao Risaldar. Maharaj told him to leave the place. Vitthalrao said, "Prabhu, I obeyed your order and sent all other souls at the other place, but please I request you to let me live here." Maharaj Shree permitted him to stay in underground space. Ganpatrao became happy and gifted the entire wado to Vaishnav community. Ther are khambhati locks toady also.

Extras:
- There was one Kharivav near Head post office building which was abolished from the earth. There is no evidence of that available anywhere. Only the name of Kharivav of that road is in existence.
- The area of Ahmedavadi pole and its outside was known as 'Piplagate'.
- There was tram running by horses. The tracks of tram were found at the time of digging \ Vadi area. There were 2 more horses joined from mota davakhana to walk through the slope at Kothi area.

SOME IMPORTANT INCIDENTS DURING SAYAJI REIGN:
1863: Shree Kashirao Gaekwad became the father of Sayajirao in Nasik District

1875: Due to overthrowing of Malharrao Gaekwad, an adopted son of Shree Khnaderao Gaekwad, Sir Sayajirao ruled the regin

1877: Death of a father of Shree Kashirao Gaekwad

1879: Maharaja dedicated the Kamatibaug to the public

1879: Foundation of Vadodara College by Maharaja

1880: Marriage with Maharani Chimnabai I

1881: Complete management rights of State given to Sayajirao

1883: Birth of Fatehsinhrao

1885: Inauguration of Ajwa Water Works by Sayajirao

1885: Death of Maharani Chimnabai I

1885: Marriage with Maharani Chimnabai II

1886: A Big hospital named Countes of Dafrin Hospital was opened up by LoardDafrin

1887: Sayajirao went to Europe for the first time due to ill health.

1887: Queen Victoria bestowed with the award GCSI

1888: Birth of Prince Jaysinhrao

1890: Establishment of Kalabhawan

1890: Birth of Prince Shivajirao

1890: Building of Laxmi Vilas Palace

1892: Ajwa Water Works was opened up for public

1892: Birth of Princess Indira Raje

1892: Election element in Baroda city

1893: Mandatory Education experimented in Amreli

1893: Born of Prince Dhairyasheelrao

1894: Investigation of Bapat Commission and Shree Bapat was recommended to give punishment

1895: Shree Bapat was proved to be innocent but was not given a job to respect the commission

1897: A Diamond Jubilee of Queen Victoria

1898: Death of Jamnabai, Widow of Shree Khnaderao, who adopted Sayajirao

1898: Plag disease found for the first time in Baroda
1899: Sayajivihar club was inaugurated
1899–90: Drought
1900: Opening of Orsang Irrigation Water Works
1901: Death of Queen Victoria
1902: Hindi Industrial Council was opened up in Ahmedabad by Sayajirao
1902: Establishment of elected gram panchayat
1904: Establishment of Regional panchayats
1904: Justice and administrative works were differentiated
1904: Hindi Social Council was headed by Sayajirao
1905: Establishment of elected towns
1905: Establishment of Cooperative Societies
1906: Sayajirao delivered the initial speech in Hindi Industrial Council
1906: Mandatory Education was entered in the entire state
1907: Legislative establishment to advice Government
1907: Celebration of Raupya Mahotsav for giving full rights to Sayajirao
1908: Opening of Bank of Baroda
1908: Birth of Prince Pratapsinhraj
1908: Death of Fatehsinhrao Gaekwad
1909: Viceroy Minto in Baroda
1910: Opening of Library in Baroda
1911: Foundation of Patan Water Works
1911: Male Education System School was founded in Baroda
1911: Appointment as President of 'First Universal Resis Congress'
1912: Opening up of Bhadaran Water Works
1913: Marriage of Prince Jaysinhrao
1913: Marriage of Princess Indira Raje
1913: Marriage of Prince Shivajirao
1914: World war between England, Russia, France and Germany
1914: First Baroda State Cooperative Council was opened up

1914–18: Sayajirao Government helped to British Government exceeding Rs. 1 Crore during world war
1915: Opening up of Patan Water Works and Maternity home
1916: Establishment of Baroda State Community
1917: Death of Shree Anandrao Gaekwad
1918: Opening up of Akhil Bharat Untouchability Nivaran Parishad
1918: Award of GCII
1918: Enfluenza in entire Baroda State
1918: End of Worldwar
1919: Death of Shivajirao
1919: Foundation of Goya Railway Workshop
1922: Princess Indira Raje became a widow
1923: Death of Prince Jaysinhrao
1926: Foundation of Kirti Mandir
1926: Golden Jubilee celebration of Sayajirao Regnal
1926: Opening up of Okha Port
1926: Opening up of Shree Pilajirao Orphanage
1927: Celebration of Sayaji triple century
1927: Danger Flood in Baroda State and Gujarat
1927: Generous help of Sayajirao during flood
1928: Inauguration of Visnagar Water works
1929: Marriage of Children less than age of 8 years became illegal, and punishment made severe for that
1929: Marriage of Prince Pratapsinhraje with Maharani Shantadevi
1930: Opening of Pratappura Lake
1933: Opening up of The Indian Oriental Conference
1934: Rule passed against Racism
1934: Succession rights of Hindu ladies made broad
1934: Death of Sampatrao Gaekwad
1935: Completed 60 years of Sayaji Regal

1936: Opening up of Kirti Mandir

1936: Started celebration of Hirak Mahotsav

1936: End of Hirak Mahotsav with opening up of statue of Sayajirao by Bikaner King opposite to Baroda railway station

1936: Sayajirao went to Europe

GALLERY OF BARODA

Makarpura Palace – 1

Makarpura Palace Gate

GALLERY OF BARODA • **97**

Makarpura Palace - 2

Makarpura Palace – Inside

Suryanarayan Temple

Hazira - Maqbara

Muharram Festival Procession

Maharaja School

Khanderao Temple

British Residency at Baroda

Nazarbag Palace – 2

Cenotaphs of Maharaja Sayajirao 1st & Fhattesing 1st

Laheripura Road

GALLERY OF BARODA • 103

Laheripura Gate

Motibag Palace

Bhadra Kacheri

Elephant Fight – Aggad Ground

GALLERY OF BARODA • 105

Pani Gate Street

Malakhambh

Palace at Makarpura (West)

Makarpura Palace Garden Bridge

New Makarpura Palace Hall

Makarpura Palace Garden

Chapaner Gate

Yeoteshwar Temple

GALLERY OF BARODA ♦ 109

Old Bridge on Vishwamitri

Hanging Bridge

Kamatibag

Band Stand

State Guest House - Kamatibag

Lakshmi Vilas Palace

View of the Regal Lakshmi Vilas Palace

Lakshmi Vilas Palace

Lakshmi Vilas Palace – Backside

Lakshmi Vilas Palace - Inside

Lakshmi Vilas Palace – Gate

GALLERY OF BARODA ♦ 115

Ganesh Festival in Lakshmi Vilas Palace

Nawalakhi Well at Palace

Kamnath Mahadev Temple

Khanderao Market

GALLERY OF BARODA • 117

Boat House

Science College

SayajiVihar Club

Kala Bhavan

Baroda College

Baroda College – Dom

Baroda College Hall – Wall Paintings

Kothi Office

Nyaya Mandir – Front Gate

Nyaya Mandir

Central Jail

Ajwa Dam

Female Education Class

GALLERY OF BARODA • 125

Baroda Museum

Front Part of the Baroda Museum

Anglo Vernacular School

Swami Narayan Temple

GALLERY OF BARODA • 127

Sursagar

Bird View of Sursagar

Military Offices at Baroda

Indumati Mahal

Raopura Street

Prince Palace

Baroda State Railway Headquarter

Maharani Chimanabai Tower

Goya Gate

Zuma Masjid

New Lehripura Gate

JumadadaAkhada

GALLERY OF BARODA • 133

Shivmahal Palace

Kirti Mandir

134 • GALLERY OF BARODA

New Kala Bhavan (Technical Institute)

Kala Ghoda

Vithal Mandir – Inside

Sarkarwada

GALLERY OF COINS

138 • GALLERY OF COINS

Copper Coins

Gold Coins

GALLERY OF COINS • 139

Silver Coins